"...Will He Find Faith On Earth?"

Luke 18:8

True Stories to Inspire Faith

By Jacqueline E. Goin

1

"…Will He Find Faith On Earth?"

Cover photo courtesy of NASA/NOAA/DoD, a high definition image of our planet earth, from data collected by the Suomi NPP satellite.

Names are sometimes changed to protect the privacy of the persons whose stories are in this book.

This book is dedicated to the Most Holy
Trinity:
God the Father, our Creator and Father,
His Beloved Son Jesus, our Merciful Savior and
Redeemer, and
The Holy Spirit, the Spirit of Truth and our
Comforter.

It is also dedicated in honor of:
The Most Blessed Virgin Mary, the Mother of
Our Lord Jesus Christ,
and our spiritual Mother, Saint Joseph, the
foster father of Jesus,
and all the Angels and Saints who have favored
our relatives and friends
by their powerful intercession whose stories are
recorded in this book.

*"The heavens declare the glory of God,
and the firmament proclaims his handiwork."*
(Psalm 19:2)

TABLE OF CONTENTS

ACKNOWLEDGMENTS

In deepest gratitude to my pastor, Fr. George Sankoorikal (retired) and to Sister Sophia Michalenko, C.M.G.T. (deceased as of 2017), the author of The Life of Faustina Kowalska, *The Authorized Biography,* Servant Books, published by St. Anthony Messenger Press, Cincinnati, Ohio, who consented to read and edit, whatever they deemed necessary. They gave me the confidence to continue with the writing of this book.

I am also grateful for the loving support and helpful suggestions of our family, Jack Goin, Diane Schiavetti Ressa, Debbie Dolhon, Kerry Corvino, Mary Staudt and Elizabeth Furber, and our friends, Sister Victoria Michalenko, C.M.G.T, Bill Fedorich, a member of our Cenacle Prayer Group, our longtime friend, Shirley Burkart and Deacon Anthony J. Detje who assisted me in the final preparation of my manuscript before sending it on to the publisher.

Special thanks go to my husband Ed, whose encouragement meant so much to me and to whom I could always go and find the better way of saying things.

How can I close this page without expressing my deep appreciation to Mary Battersby wife of Deacon Lawrence Battersby, who said to me, (many years ago), "Jackie, you should write a book, you have so many stories."

PREFACE

Since I have written many books about the saints you may be surprised that I don't particularly like devotional literature, preferring liturgical prayer and charismatic prayer! So when I received "True Stories to Inspire Faith" by Jacqueline E. Goin to review I thought, "Well, I will skim the book and give her ideas for publishers who specialize in the genre of devotional spirituality."

Surprise! I love this book. Let me explain. Some books about minor and big miracles coming from devotional practices I find too pushy.

Or, some devotional books make it seem as if the locutions from the alleged, not yet finally approved, are more important than reading Scripture or the spiritual writings of the doctors of the Church. It happens that I went to Medjugorje and did have what seemed like visions from God, and I read the messages each month but, for me they don't trump the readings at daily Mass or the reading of Sacred Scripture, which Mary, the Mother of Jesus, does recommend in her messages.

By contrast, Jacqueline Goin's book of stories about graces and miracles from devotional prayer and apparition sites are written in a lovely personal style that is engaging and gently inviting of trying a devotion we might have overlooked. And the stories truly are exciting, astounding and heart-warming.

So, I recommend "Will He Find Faith on Earth?" not only for lovers of all devotional prayers old and new, but also for those like me who love some, but don't practice others yet. And I would even give it to skeptics who might need a second look at the rosary, or the scapular, or a pilgrimage, when in dire need for a healing or for simply, to inspire greater faith.

Ronda Chervin, Ph.D., Emerita Professor of Philosophy, Holy Apostles College and Seminary, Cromwell CT, and author of some 50 books on lay spirituality and the saints.

FOREWORD

How and Why I Wrote This Book

About fifteen years ago, an English teacher and the wife of a deacon, said to me, "Jackie, you should write a book, you have so many stories." Today, January 4, 2007, I am beginning that book.

This past September, my husband Ed and I went to see friends in Cape Cod, Massachusetts. In the morning, we went to Mass at the local Catholic Church. When the deacon gave the general intercessions one of them was, *"That the Church may be filled with people of strong faith, willing to share their faith stories for the building up of the kingdom of God,"* then the congregation answered, *"Lord, hear our prayer."* When I heard this, I was amazed! It's the first time I've ever heard that particular intercession and I've heard many, having gone to daily Mass for many years.

When Mass was over I went to see the deacon at the back of the church. I asked him if he would please give me a copy of the intercession. I told him I wanted to write a book of true stories about God, and I also told him what my friend, the English teacher had said. The deacon, while pointing his finger at me, shook his hand adamantly and said, "*Write that book!!*" He then ripped out the typewritten page from the notebook he held that had the intercessions on it and handed it to me. We spoke a little more and then he repeated exactly as he did before and said again, "*Write that book!!*" A couple of days later I noticed the bottom of the page. The next day was Saint Padre Pio's feast day, September 23rd.

This really moved me because a number of years before, while on a retreat entitled, "The Holy Spirit in the Life of Padre Pio," I learned that Padre Pio said, "*I have made a pact with the Lord: I will take my place at the gate to paradise, but I shall not enter until I have seen the last of my spiritual children enter."* We were told we could write to San Giovanni Rotundo in Italy, where the saint had lived and died, asking to be accepted as a spiritual son or daughter of St. Pio, which I did very soon after I got home from the retreat. Sometime later my husband also became a spiritual son of the Padre. I took the fact that the next day was St. Pio's feast day as another confirmation to "Write that book!

And so it begins. I hope this journey finds you blessed.

Jacqueline E. Goin

GOD HAS A PLAN

When I was a teenager one of my mother's friends, gave her a Miraculous Medal which she had received from a customer at the beauty parlor she owned. My mother offered it to me, and I've been wearing a Miraculous Medal ever since. I know in my heart that I have received many undeserved graces throughout my life from our Blessed Mother.

In September of 1952, the Korean War was in progress. Ed, whom I had dated for about six months until I decided to break up with him, went down to the draft board in New York City to request an early enlistment. When he called to tell me of this, I nonchalantly asked him, "Aren't you going to come to see me for my birthday?" (My birthday was the following weekend and I wanted to see him before he left for the service). When we hung up the phone, I cried hysterically, and in my heart I knew how very much I loved him.

Of course, he came for my birthday and brought me a radio for my room at Belleview Nursing School where I was studying to be a nurse. Soon he was off to basic training in Camp

Breckinridge, Kentucky. The letters flew back and forth almost daily. When Ed came home on leave the following March he asked me to marry

him, after a not-so-subtle hint from me, when he got out of the Army. By then I would have only one more year of nursing school to finish and I enthusiastically said, "I'd love to." We went shopping together for an engagement ring. A friend of mine knew a jeweler and Ed and I picked out a beautiful ring together. My mother gave us a lovely engagement party in the three-room apartment which she and I shared. My sister was already married and down in Alabama with her husband Charlie who was in the Air Force. How happy Ed and I were!

Before long, Ed's leave time was over. He was sent to Fort Lewis, in the state of Washington, soon to be shipped overseas to Korea. He arrived in Korea on April 18, 1953, and was a soldier in the infantry. He wrote to me almost every day and I did the same. How I looked forward to his wonderful letters! He was very accepting of his time in the Army. His encampment was in the valley between "Old Baldy" and "Pork Chop Hill," two famous Korean War battlegrounds.

Then it happened. On July 4, 1953, while out on patrol, one of the members of his platoon stepped on a land mine and Ed was wounded. I didn't find out about what happened until the following weekend. My mother, Evelyn Mee, had come to see me at nursing school and brought her sister, my Aunt Marie with her. This was July, and she hadn't come to see me since September when she helped me settle into my dorm room. (I was home almost every weekend). I enjoyed showing my aunt around, especially since she was a registered nurse. We then went down to the local luncheonette for a soda.

While we were there my friend Pat, another student nurse, came to inform me that there was a call for me from Ed's mother, Betty Goin, at the nursing school. Immediately I got scared. This was the first time Ed's mother phoned me and I just knew it had to be bad news. I anxiously went over to the public phone in the luncheonette and called her back. She spoke very calmly to me and after exchanging greetings she asked me if I had received any letters from

Eddie lately. I nervously said, "Yes, a couple of days ago," and then she asked, "When was it dated, Jackie?" My heart dropped as I inquired, "Why?" She answered, "Oh, nothing," but then added she'd like to come down to see me. I just knew something happened to Ed and I didn't want to wait to find out what it was. I told her I'd like to come up to see her that evening and she said, "Okay." I hung up the phone and then cried hysterically as I walked back to the booth where my mother, aunt, and Pat were sitting.

When they heard about the conversation that took place between Ed's mother and me, my mother and aunt willingly agreed to go with me by subway up to the Bronx to Ed's parents' apartment to find out what happened to Ed. How good God was to me to inspire my mother and aunt to come to see me and be with me that night! On the train ride from Manhattan to the Bronx, my mother and aunt each had an arm around my waist to comfort me.

When we arrived at the apartment, my mother walked down the hall ahead of me to ask Ed's mother what happened. Then my mother turned to me to tell me the best news I could have heard. Ed was slightly wounded. Of course this wasn't good news, but it was a relief compared to any other news we might have heard about him. My anxiety left me and a hopeful peace enveloped me. After spending some time with Ed's mother and father we all made our way back home.

After being wounded, Ed was flown by helicopter from Korea to Tokyo General Hospital in Japan. He had shrapnel, from the explosion of the mine, in the back of his head close to his left ear and in his thigh. His condition was officially changed from slightly, to seriously, wounded. The doctor told him that if the shrapnel had gone into his head one quarter of an inch more he would have died. He also told him that if the shrapnel in his thigh went in horizontally rather than vertically, he would be limping for the rest of his life.

The doctors decided that to attempt to remove the shrapnel in his head would be more dangerous than leaving it where it was. They also didn't remove the piece of metal that lodged in his leg.

I still have a letter from Ed dated July 11, 1953, which he wrote to me from the hospital on American National Red Cross stationery. In it he said, "I think the Blessed Mother was looking after me that night." When Ed was a little boy, in addition to Sunday Mass, his mother often took him to the special devotions that were held in their church in honor of Our Lady. Ed was always faithful to his religious duties. Besides going to Mass on Sundays and Holy Days he went to confession about every three weeks. This was one of the things I loved about him.

At this point, Ed and I can't remember for sure if he was wearing, when he was wounded, a Cross medal (commonly known as a four-way cross) which I had given him, that includes the Miraculous, the Scapular, St. Joseph and St. Christopher medals. But I vaguely remember asking him, "Where is your medal?" when he received a package later on from overseas that contained some items that were left there when he got wounded. He then assumed they must have removed it at one point after he was injured. One thing is for sure, he certainly was protected from an even more serious injury that night of July 4, 1953.

While in the hospital, Ed wrote me that he had double vision and difficulty in hearing. When he came home he told us that one of the men in the hospital was playing a record and although Ed could see the record spinning, he couldn't hear any sound coming from it at all at that point. One day the Army band came to entertain the patients in the hospital. Ed looked down into the courtyard and heard that they were playing: "When the Saints Come Marching In!" Praise God!! His hearing was slowly returning!

Before long, Ed was transferred from Tokyo General to Walter Reed Army Hospital in Washington, D.C. Ed's parents, aunt, uncle and their two children drove down to see him. My mother offered to go with me to see Ed. It was so good to have her with me on that long trip to Washington and back. Since we had no car in those days, we took the train from Pennsylvania Station in N.Y.C. to D.C. My mother's brother, Bob and his wife Jeanne who lived in nearby Bethesda, Maryland, lovingly welcomed us to stay with them and their two children at the time, Bobby and Michael, while we were visiting Ed. How anxious I was to see him and make sure he was okay! When we finally arrived at Walter Reed I was shocked to see how thin he looked, and also how different, with only peach fuzz for hair covering his head, but it was wonderful just to see him alive, walking, and on the road to recovery.

Eventually Eddie was asked where he would like to spend the remainder of his time in the service. He answered, "Fordham Road Recruiting Station." (That was located in the Bronx, N.Y. not far from where I lived). Since only two servicemen were stationed there at a time, they asked him for another choice. He mentioned Camp Kilmer in New Jersey and that's where he was transferred.

Since he was now back home in the states, I chose not to continue my nursing career. We decided to get married earlier than planned, at a Nuptial Mass at St. Nicholas of Tolentine, my parish church, on November 28, 1953. The day before our wedding, in preparation for receiving the Sacrament of  Marriage, (which we receive whether or not we have a Nuptial Mass), I took the subway to St. Francis of Assisi Church in New York where confessions were heard for many hours every day and made my confession. We had very little money but a lot of faith in God, who never let us down, as we looked forward to raising a family. Our first child, John Francis (Jack), was born on October 11, 1954, at Camp Kilmer Army Hospital. How happy we were to welcome our son! From then on, I've often said, "I did all my nursing at home."

Jack started walking when he was eleven months old. One day I was washing dishes at the kitchen sink and Jack came to me and touched me to get my attention. I turned around and there he was, his face having already turned blue

So big and safe!

because he was not able to breathe. I quickly opened his mouth and saw that he had a lollipop wrapper all crunched up and caught in his throat. I instinctively did, what I've since read I wasn't supposed to do, and reached into his mouth to try to grab the wrapper to remove it. It didn't work. I desperately turned him upside down and cried out loudly in great agony as I looked up, "God help me!" I pounded on his back, and thank God, the wrapper popped out. Then Jack did something he never did before. He kept kissing me all over my face. He knew I had helped him and showed me his gratitude profoundly, even at eleven months old! Yes, I had taught him to blow a kiss to me and others when asked, but he never did it on his own. It was amazing! Thank you, Lord, for answering my prayer that day, so many years ago.

I never thought about it until I wrote this story about our son Jack, but yes, I was wearing my Miraculous Medal that day, as always, since I never take it off. It makes me wonder, how many times Mary has helped me without my even realizing it? Thank you Mother, for your constant help!

THE ORIGIN OF THE
MIRACULOUS MEDAL

On the night of July 18, 1830, Sister Catherine Labouré, a 24-year-old novice of the Daughters of Charity, had an apparition of the Virgin Mary. A novice is one who has entered a religious community and is preparing to be received as a permanent member. Sister Catherine and the Blessed Virgin spoke familiarly for two hours. This all took place in the chapel at the Motherhouse of the Sisters located in Paris on Rue du Bac.

On November 27, the Mother of Jesus appeared for the second time to Sister Catherine asking her to have a medal struck according to the vision she was being shown. As she contemplated the apparition she heard the words, "Have a medal struck upon this model. Those who wear it will receive great graces, especially if they wear it around the neck." There was an oval frame surrounding Our Lady who was standing on a globe, with her foot crushing a serpent's head. From her outstretched hands were beautiful rays of light, symbolic of graces obtained by those who ask for them.

Around the outer edge of the medal was

the prayer: "Oh Mary conceived without sin, pray for us who have recourse to thee." On the back of the vision of the medal there was the letter M and a bar surmounted by a Cross, a reminder of Christ's suffering and death. Under these symbols were the Heart of Jesus crowned with thorns and the Heart of Mary pierced with a sword. Encircling all were twelve stars.

In a previous visit, Our Lady had said: "Come to the foot of the altar. Here graces will be bestowed." From Mary, Sister Catherine learned how to pray: "When I go to the Chapel, I place myself before the good God. I say to him: "Lord, here I am." If He gives me something I am pleased. If He gives me nothing, I thank Him also because I do not deserve anything. I recount my pains and joys....and I listen." When I read this about Sister Catherine I was very moved by her humility before the Lord, and by her love of God.

With the approval of the Church, the first medals were made in 1832 and were distributed in Paris. It was originally called the medal of the Immaculate Conception. Almost immediately the blessings Mary had promised began to be bestowed on those who wore her medal with devotion. Miracles of grace, health, conversion, and peace were given. Within a short period of time many persons throughout the world started to wear the medal. It became known by the people as the "Miraculous Medal" because of the many favors received by those who wore it. It is important to have the medal blessed by a priest or a deacon.

Sister Catherine lived a life of prayer and service to the poor. She was canonized a saint by Pope Pius XII in 1947. Her body lies incorrupt (miraculously preserved), and is enshrined in the chapel of the Motherhouse of the Daughters of Charity in Paris. The body of the Co-founder of the Daughters of Charity, St. Louise de Marillac is also enshrined in the chapel.

Those interested in purchasing a Miraculous Medal or learning more about the life of St. Catherine Labouré may contact the National Shrine of Our Lady of the Miraculous Medal at the following address:

Association of the Miraculous Medal
1811 W. Saint Joseph St.
Perryville, MI 63775
1-800-264-MARY (6279)
www.amm.org

or:

The Central Association of the Miraculous
Medal
475 E. Chelten Ave.
Philadelphia, PA 19144
1-800-523-3674
www.cammonline.org

HOW THE MIRACULOUS MEDAL CHANGED MY LIFE
by Fr. John A. Harden, S.J.

One of the most memorable experiences that I ever had was with the Miraculous Medal! It changed my life.

In the fall of 1948, the year after my ordination, I was in what we call the Tertianship. This is a third year of Novitiate before taking final vows.

In October of that year, a Vincentian priest came to speak to us young Jesuit priests. He encouraged us to obtain faculties, as they are called, to enroll people in the Association of the Miraculous Medal. Among other things, he said, "Fathers, the Miraculous Medal works. Miracles have been performed by Our Lady through the Miraculous Medal."

I was not impressed by what the Vincentian priest was telling. I was not the medal-wearing kind of person and I certainly did not have a Miraculous Medal. But I thought to myself, "It does not cost anything." So I put my name down to get a four-page leaflet from the Vincentians, with the then-Latin formula for blessing Miraculous Medals and enrolling people in the Association of the Miraculous Medal. About two weeks later, I got the leaflet for blessing and enrollment, put it into my office book and forgot about it.

In February of the next year, I was sent to assist the chaplain of St. Alexis Hospital in Cleveland, Ohio. I was to be there helping the regular chaplain for two weeks. Each morning I received a list of all the patients admitted into the hospital that day. There was so many Catholics admitted that I could not visit them all as soon as they came.

Among the patients admitted was a boy about nine years old. He had been sled-riding down a hill, lost control of the sled and ran into a tree head-on. He fractured his skull and X-rays showed he had suffered severe brain damage.

After blessing the boy and consoling his parents, I was about to leave his hospital room. But then a thought came to me, "That Vincentian priest. He said, 'The Miraculous Medal works.' Now this will be a test of its alleged miraculous powers!"

I didn't have a Miraculous Medal of my own. And everyone I asked at the hospital also did not have one. But I persisted, and finally one of the nursing sisters on night duty found a

Miraculous Medal.

What I found out was that you don't just bless the medal; you have to put it around a person's neck on a chain or ribbon. So the sister-nurse found a blue ribbon for the medal, which made me feel silly. What was I doing with medals and blue ribbons?

However, I blessed the medal and had the father hold the leaflet for investing a person in the Association of the Miraculous Medal. I proceeded to recite the words of investiture. No sooner did I finish the prayer of enrolling the boy in the Association than he opened his eyes for the first time in two weeks. He saw his mother and said, "Ma, I want some ice cream." He had been given only intravenous feeding.

This Experience Changed My Life!

Then he proceeded to talk to his father and mother. After a few minutes of stunned silence, a doctor was called. The doctor examined the boy and told the parents they could give him something to eat.

The next day began a series of tests on the boy's condition. X-rays showed the brain damage was gone. Then still more tests. After three days, when all examinations showed there was complete restoration to health, the boy was released from the hospital.

This experience so changed my life that I have not been the same since. My faith in God, faith in His power to work miracles, was strengthened beyond description. Since then, of course, I have been promoting devotion to Our Lady and the use of the Miraculous Medal. The wonders she performs, provided we believe, are extraordinary.

In teaching theology over the years, I have for many semesters taught the theology of miracles. And I have an unpublished book manuscript on "The History and Theology of Miracles." My hope is to publish the manuscript in the near future.

(Note: Fr. John A. Hardon, S.J. was born on June 18, 1914 and passed away on December 30, 2000. He has been given the title "Servant of God," a title given to a deceased member of the Roman Catholic Church whose life is being *investigated as the first step towards canonization (being declared a Saint of the Church).*

THE POWERFUL INTERCESSION OF MARY
AND HER MIRACULOUS MEDAL

My sister Dot was away from the Church for almost sixty years. Since I've been in my twenties I went to the Miraculous Medal Novena with Benediction of the Most Blessed Sacrament every Monday to pray for her conversion. This I did for many years.

At one point, although I still prayed for Dot, I stopped going to novena; that is until during a visit with her and her husband Charlie, I shared with them about the healing I received at the final blessing of (St.) John Paul II at the Mass in Central Park in New York City. My sister immediately left the room and expressed her disbelief vehemently. Charlie asked me how I would explain what happened to me at that time and I answered, "It was the Holy Spirit." (You may want to read "Pope John Paul II's Visit to Central Park"). Dot soon came back into the room and apologized. I went over to her, kissed her and said, "I forgive you because I love you." When I got home I said to myself, "I better go back to novena," which I did.

Dot was an avid reader. When she told me

she read about six books a week when my husband Ed and I went to visit them in Florida where they lived after their retirement, I was astonished! When we got home I decided to send her a copy of "Heaven Is For Real" in the hopes that its message would be helpful to her. I don't recall if she made any comment on it but when I asked her if I could send her a copy of "Honey from the Rock" she said emphatically, "Don't send me any more books"!! The subtitle of "Honey from the Rock" is "Sixteen Jews Find the Sweetness of Christ."

In the meantime I had been working on my book, "Will He Find Faith on Earth?" When I finished writing it I asked Dot if she would like to read it. She said, "Send me the first chapter." I told her that I'd really like to include, "How and Why I Wrote This Book" and she reluctantly agreed. After Dot read what I sent her she said something like, "It's very nice." I said if she wanted me to send her the rest of my book to let me know. Since she didn't ask me for any more chapters I let it go.

Some time passed and for my birthday our daughter Mary, as a present to me, had a copy of my manuscript printed out with a spiraled edging on it. When I told Dot, via the phone what Mary had done I asked her if she'd like me to send it on to her for her to read. She surprised me by responding, "I'd be insulted if you didn't send it to me!" I found out later that Dot mistakenly thought that Mary had printed 100 copies for me.

As I already mentioned Dot was an avid reader and had my book finished in a short time. She sent me an email which absolutely astounded me! She loved my book! Her last sentence in her email said that she REALLY loved my book!!

About a year later Dot's health was declining and we knew, as she did also, that she didn't have many more months to live. I asked if she and Charlie would be willing to have me come to visit for about a week. They agreed it would be ok for me to make the trip. Ed was good about my leaving him home to fend for himself and so I went. It was so good to see them and I tried to help out by cooking and freezing some dinners for them to enjoy after I went back home. I mentioned the first night I was there that they both knew that I go to Mass every day but if they needed me I would forgo going. They both graciously said to go ahead because they would be ok on their own while I was gone. After Mass I told the priest my sister's situation and asked if he would be willing to come to see her. Of course he said yes. When I broached the subject with Dot she gently moved her head from side to side ever so slightly and said she didn't want to be a hypocrite. I simply answered, "Jesus is merciful." I knew I couldn't pursue it further. It was up to her.

About three weeks before Dot passed away I called her and said, "Dot, you read my book and know that the Blessed Mother is mother to us all. Dot said "yes" in agreement. And so I ventured, "Dot if I send you my Miraculous Medal would you wear it?" Dot responded, "What's that?! I shared with her that I had been wearing a Miraculous Medal ever since I was a teenager and she then answered wistfully, "Oh yes, I used to wear one when I was young." And then Dot said, "Yes." How happy I was!

I had recently asked a friend who was going overseas on pilgrimage to purchase a gold Miraculous Medal for me which she did. I never had a gold medal before but I knew my sister couldn't wear anything but gold because of her skin condition, and I already had a gold chain which I could send with the medal. I could then go back to wearing the medal I had before.

I quickly wrapped my blessed medal with the chain and sent it off to Dot. When she received the medal, she called me and said, "Jackie, it's beautiful" and thanked me for sending it.

Dot's daughter Peggy moved closer to her parents so she could help them out whenever she could. Charlie told me that Dot often fondled the medal. Peggy mentioned that when the medal fell behind Dot's neck, which happened often because she was in bed at that point for the most part, her mother asked her, "Where's my medal, where's my medal?" Finally Peggy pinned the medal to the front of my sister's gown which solved the problem. She also had a rosary on her night table which Charlie said I had given her during one of our visits to Florida which she often prayerfully clutched. Peggy told me that Dot said to her, "The Blessed Mother is helping me."

My sister passed away peacefully on the Feast of the Presentation of the Child Jesus in the Temple, February 2nd. Praise God and His Most Holy Mother Mary for the help she gave my sister Dot and all others who turn to her, by her powerful intercession with her beloved Son Jesus!

"...let us take refuge under the mantle of Mary, and she most certainly will not reject us, but will secure our salvation." (St. Gertrude)

On Valentine's Day, Ed wanted to take me out for dinner. When we called the restaurant to make a reservation we weren't able to get a table until 9:00 p.m., an hour later than we had hoped for but we accepted it. When the waiter came over to take our order he asked if I had received a flower yet. I answered no I hadn't and he went off to get me one. I turned to Ed and said, "If he brings me a rose I'm going to cry." I hadn't previously told Ed after my sister passed away I prayed to St. Thérèse, "If my sister is ok (meaning saved) please send me a rose."

When our waiter came back he didn't have one flower, he had two flowers and they were both roses and they were beautiful!! I then noticed that all the tables that were occupied had one rose on them which were evidently for all the ladies who came in that night for Valentine's Day dinner. And so I asked our waiter if any of the other ladies received two roses and he said, "No, only you."

When the maître'd came over to our table, I asked her if anyone else received two roses. She also said "no". I was really amazed since there were a lot of dinners served that night. I was so grateful to St. Thérèse for answering my prayer.

After a week or two I realized, if I had been given only one rose as every other lady I could have dismissed it as an answer to prayer because all the ladies had one rose but I had received two!! Thank you St. Thérèse!

HOUSE FOR SALE!

A year after my husband and I got married, we bought our first home in New Jersey in a housing development. There was another development of homes being built not too far away but they were much larger than the one we decided on. We already had our first baby and didn't want to be worried about paying off a larger mortgage on the bigger house, in case we had an increase in our family as we had hoped for. And so, we started out with a small Cape Cod with two bedrooms, one bath, a kitchen, living room and expansion attic. We were able to meet the payments on this house with no problem.

After five years and two more children, we were ready to move back to New York, closer to our family. My husband and I made a novena to St. Jude, Saint of the Impossible, so called because he prays very efficaciously for the most difficult situations. We had no trouble selling our home, and then bought our first home in Yonkers, New York. We were very grateful to St. Jude for his help in selling our house so quickly.

We lived in the Yonkers home for about

five years, and during this time we asked our pastor if he would come to our home and consecrate our family to the Sacred Heart of Jesus. At the entrance to the living room we had a picture of Jesus with his Sacred Heart which our pastor blessed. We all knelt down as Father prayed the prayers of consecration. How good it was to know we were consecrated in a special way to the Sacred Heart.

Soon we decided to look for a larger home again, closer to our parish church and school, as we were now looking forward to the fifth addition to our family. And so, we made another novena to St. Jude. But this time our prayers were not answered right away. How difficult it is when you have a young family and you receive a phone call that someone would like to come to see the house! You quickly run around straightening the towels in the bathroom, picking up toys, collapsing the playpen that our daughter Mary was still using, so the living room would look larger, the house look neat, etc., etc.

After three months of this I decided to make a novena to the Holy Spirit. "Oh Holy Spirit," I prayed, "There must be someone who would like this house." Every hour for the next nine hours I said prayers to the Holy Spirit from my novena book. The next day a couple came to see our house and bought it that very day! Praise be to the Holy Spirit! They must have liked it because they lived there for many years.

This made me think that the reason St. Jude didn't answer our prayers right away was because he wanted me to pray to and have confidence in, the Holy Spirit! Sometime before, an elderly woman in our parish had given me the booklet containing the novena prayers to the Holy Spirit. I will be forever grateful to her.

When our daughter Elizabeth was born we decided to ask our parish priest to consecrate our family to the Immaculate Heart of Mary after her baptism which was about three weeks later. Now we had the joy of knowing we were consecrated to the two hearts, of Jesus and Mary.

Prayers to the Holy Spirit

Come, Holy Spirit, fill the hearts of Your faithful, and enkindle in them the fire of Your love. Send forth Your Spirit and they shall be created. And You shall renew the face of the earth.

Let us pray.

O God, who did instruct the hearts of the faithful by the light of the Holy Spirit, grant us in the same Spirit to be truly wise, and ever to rejoice in His consolation, through Jesus Christ our Lord. Amen. Come Holy Spirit, come by means of the powerful intercession of the Immaculate Heart of Mary, Your well beloved spouse.

Note: Anyone wanting to purchase a booklet containing a Novena and Prayers to the Holy Spirit may obtain one by contacting:

Discount Catholic Products
27212 471st Ave., Harrisburg, SD 57032
1-877-700-5378
service@discountcatholicproducts.com

MY GRANDPARENTS

I was very close to my grandparents, Elizabeth and Robert Wilkes. Because my mother was a widow, whenever I got sick, which was quite often (every two or three weeks, when I was young), she took me to their apartment by taxi before she went to work so they could take care of me. My grandparents had thirteen children, ten of whom survived through adulthood. My aunts were like sisters to me and I experienced firsthand the beauty of a large family.

As a young child I saw my grandparents' devotion and great faith in God. They both went to daily Mass, and while I was recuperating, I often went along with them. Otherwise, one of them would go to an earlier Mass so that I wouldn't be left alone. After Mass, my grandmother would pray the Stations of the Cross. If she didn't get that done in the morning she would go in the afternoon to the church, which was diagonally across the street, to "do her Stations," as she put it.

I still remember a day when my grandmother and I were leaving the church after Mass. As we passed the poor box my grandmother opened her purse and put a dime in the slot. "I can never pass a poor box," she told me, "without putting something in it." What an example that was for me, and how profoundly it affected me!

After dinner each night, my grandfather would sit down in his chair in the living room to read the Bible. One day he told me he read the whole Bible through two times! One evening I saw my grandmother kneeling down by her bed praying her Rosary. She prayed it every day. One of my aunts told me that my grandfather did the same.

Grandpa was the organist at St. Peter's Church on Barclay Street in New York City for about 50 years. St. Peter's is the oldest Catholic Church in New York. It is also the Church where Saint Elizabeth Ann Seton was received on August 14, 1805, as a convert from the Episcopal faith that she grew up in. She founded the Sisters of Charity, now called the Daughters of Charity, in 1809.

My grandfather also taught music at a couple of Catholic schools. He wrote three oratorios, one on Moses, another on Joseph of the book of Genesis, and one on Mary Magdalen, in addition to other church music. After my grandmother passed away in her 70s, he lived alone, taking care of himself and was often visited by his children until he became a little unsteady on his feet. Because he had five flights of stairs to navigate up to his apartment, my Aunt Margie and Uncle Bill asked him to come and live with them and their family. He continued to go to daily Mass at their local church which was close to their home, and he played bridge once a week until he suffered a stroke, at age 87, and was hospitalized.

The day before he had the stroke, my Aunt Alma, who lived in Maine, came to New York to visit her father. She told me they had a beautiful day. They had lunch together at the house. Whenever my grandfather had company for lunch, he would go to the local deli and buy cold cuts, potato salad and a tomato for slicing. In addition he always had a nice dessert to offer and a box of candy to choose a piece or two from. A glass of wine, ginger ale or a cup of tea was always offered too. He would help put everything out and also shared with the clean-up. After lunch he acquiesced to Alma's request to play her favorite song on his piano, Chopin's Waltz in C# Minor. She loved hearing him play. Everything he played he did with great expression. It was truly a joy to listen to him. After a while it was time to leave and Alma went home so happy she had this special visit with her Daddy, especially when she received a call that night that her Dad had suffered a stroke.

I offered to go and stay with my grandfather during the night hours the first night he was in the hospital. His condition was very serious and I was really afraid. On my way to the hospital I thought to myself, "Suppose he dies while I'm there?" Then I realized, "If that should happen, it would be an honor and a privilege to be present at my grandfather's death."

I brought with me a bottle of holy water. Grandpa always had a holy water font in his bedroom which he used to bless himself every day. There was also one in the kitchen. I also brought with me a picture of the Sacred Heart of Jesus, a small framed one, which I placed on his night table when I arrived. My grandparents always had a large picture of the Sacred Heart in their bedroom.

My grandfather did not recognize that I was there. He was probably in a coma, and he was breathing very heavily. At one point during the night I was suddenly aware of a heavenly aroma in the room. I looked around for flowers that could possibly be causing this wonderful scent. After finding no flowers, I went out in the hall to see if possibly a door had been opened where they had some flowers. Not seeing any, I went back to the room and realized that it must be Our Lord, the Blessed Mother, or St. Thérèse who had come to help my grandfather in his last agony. After the aroma had left the room and my grandfather started breathing more heavily, I asked the nurse to call my Aunt Margie. Very soon four of my aunts and an uncle arrived.

About seven in the morning his condition worsened and they called the emergency team to the room. One of the nurses happened to accidentally knock over the picture of the Sacred Heart. As it hit the table my grandfather jumped! It has been said that the hearing is the last to go, and this was proof to us that he could hear us praying for him. A Capuchin priest, one of the hospital chaplains, came into the room and blessed him with the Most Holy Eucharist. As they worked on my grandfather, I blessed him with the holy water I had brought, and as I did so the most heavenly, boyish smile came over his face, and then, after a few more breaths, he died. What a privilege it was to be there with him, and what a consolation it was to us to witness his beautiful smile just before he passed away.

"He who fears the LORD will have a happy end; even on the day of his death he will be blessed."
(Sirach 1:11)

A CHRISTMAS GIFT

When I was a young child in grade school, my grandmother asked me if I would like to set up their nativity set since Christmas was soon arriving. Of course, I was happy to do so. And this I gladly did for the next few years. It was such a beautiful crèche. Besides Mary, Joseph and the Infant Jesus, it contained the shepherds, the Magi, some sheep, a donkey, an ox and even a camel. It was always set up on an oval table covered with straw in a corner of their dining room. In back of the crèche my grandfather set up a lovely dark blue curtain behind which was a star that lit up through the curtain whenever the light was turned on in the stable. It was very beautiful and inspiring.

As my grandparents advanced in age, my grandmother asked my grandfather if he would purchase an infant Jesus to use in place of the nativity set they had cherished for so many years. There were a number of religious gift shops on Barclay Street in New York City near St. Peter's Church where he was the organist. Well, one day my grandfather came home with the most beautiful infant Jesus you'd ever want to see! It was so realistic, quite large, and had a manger for the infant to be placed in. The full nativity scene was to be retired, and to be given eventually to the family of one of their ten children.

Whenever I visited my grandparents at Christmas, my grandmother would always ask me, "Did you see my infant?" Then I would go to the spot where he was placed to see her statue of the infant Jesus which she obviously loved so much.

A year or so after my husband and I married, I asked my grandfather to buy a few pieces of the nativity scene for us so that we could build upon it every year. Barclay Street had a beautiful selection of statutes at that time. We were very happy with what my grandfather selected for us. Eventually, after my mother passed away, we had two nativity sets, hers and ours. My grandparents had also passed away and their infant went to my Aunt Margie. At Christmas we displayed my mother's crèche in our living room, and our crèche was displayed downstairs in front of the fireplace which was on a wall opposite the main entrance to our home.

One Advent, before we had the opportunity to set up our family's nativity scenes, our cleaning girl, let's call her Maria, told me, "Mrs. Goin, I saw the most beautiful infant on display in a store window at Getty Square (which is in downtown Yonkers). I just **had** to order it for you, but you have to promise me you will use it." While she was saying this I was thinking to myself, "I don't need another infant, (I already had two)." But how could I hurt her feelings? Of course I thanked her and promised to use it.

In a couple of weeks, Maria presented me with a box containing the infant she had purchased for us. I opened the box and couldn't believe what I was seeing! It was the exact same infant that my grandparents had! I was so thrilled! The only difference was that this infant was a little smaller, but the size was perfect as far as I was concerned. I thanked Maria profusely. What a wonderful gift! I felt that my grandparents had a hand in inspiring her with the desire to order one for us. And now, during the Christmas season when we have company I sometimes ask, "Did you see my infant?"

Many years later I had the joy of lending our infant to the outdoor nativity scene of our parish church since the infant that came with their set was missing. What a gift it was to personally place our infant in the manger in time for Christmas Eve Mass celebration! When the

Christmas season was over our infant was returned to us, since a new one was to be purchased for our parish for the following year. And so we do have our special infant with us again. I remember very lovingly and gratefully placing him in his manger the following Christmas. It was so wonderful to have him back!

THE MASS AND THE SACRAMENTS

I didn't always go to daily Mass, but I didn't miss going on Sunday and Holy Days unless I was sick. I forced myself to go to confession and then receive Holy Communion during the Easter time and was always happy I did. I usually did the same for Christmas but other than that, at Sunday Mass I didn't go up to receive Communion. I made a Spiritual Communion when it was time for the priest to distribute the Holy Eucharist, and would say within myself, "Dear Jesus, I believe in you, I hope in you, I love you, I'm sorry for all my sins, and although I cannot now receive You bodily, please come spiritually into my heart. I treat Thee as though You have already come. Sever the chains that hold me back from Thee. Free me oh beauteous God from all but Thee and bind me evermore close to Thee. Never permit me to be separated from Thee."

I once said to my grandfather, "I don't like going to confession." His answer to me was, "Nobody does." But, he told me that he went every two weeks in order to receive all the indulgences of the Church for the holy souls in purgatory. (The traditional norm for going to confession, receiving Holy Communion, and praying for the intentions of the pope, in order to gain a plenary indulgence, was 8 days before or after doing the prescribed work.)

In the Great Jubilee Year 2000, the Apostolic Penitentiary relaxed this norm to "several days (about 20) before or after the indulgenced act." This norm of "about 20 days" remains in effect, since it was contained under the "General remarks on indulgences," and not under those specific to the Jubilee Indulgence. Indulgences, plenary or partial, may be gained for ourselves or for the souls of the deceased.

In the early 1960's Pope John XXIII granted indulgences to everyone who offers his daily work to God in the morning, whether manual or intellectual, using any formula of prayer. A plenary indulgence under the usual conditions or a partial one may be gained as often as, with contrite heart they offer their present work at hand, with any formula of prayer. More information about obtaining indulgences can be found on the internet at: Indulgences-General Conditions-EWTN.

When our children started to go to school, I wanted to be a good example for them. And so I made the effort to receive the sacraments more frequently. I found a very patient priest who was very helpful in the confessional. And although I was still nervous about going, I was always happy I did.

I still remember one time, many years ago, as I approached the church and felt particularly nervous, I offered my nervousness in union with Our Lord's agony in the garden. Somehow I immediately felt better and found out by experience Our Lord's graciousness of helping us to carry our crosses whenever we unite our sufferings to His.

I have personally come to believe that our crosses become easier to carry when we *willingly* carry them out of love for Our Lord because it is then that He is there sharing our burden.

At one time I shared with our Cenacle prayer group that when I go to confession I hold my Rosary and I ask our Blessed Mother, St. Joseph, St. Padre Pio, and St. Thérèse to come in with me to help me make a good confession. Upon hearing this, one of our members said, "It must get awfully crowded in there," and everyone roared laughing, including myself. When on pilgrimage some years ago, I related this story in confession to the very special priest who was our chaplain. He said, "There's room for many more."

When our children were in school I started going to daily Mass. There are a few beautiful families in our area who obviously home school their children and bring them to Mass every day. What a treat it was to see Katera, at age two, filing into the pew with the rest of her family, only to rush back in front of them, going once more into the center aisle, genuflecting, making the sign of the cross, and then going back to her seat! Those who happened to notice her were full of smiles, and I'm sure Our Lord himself couldn't help but join us.

When we consider Whom we are receiving, the sacrifices we may need to make in order to receive Our Lord in Holy Communion are worth it. I agree with St. John Vianney who said, "The priest holds the key to the treasures of life." (The Mass and the Sacraments)

The following prayer has been known for many years and is prayed by many to assist the souls in purgatory to attain their heavenly goal, and also to benefit the souls of the living. It has been stated that Our Lord said that very many souls would be released from Purgatory whenever the prayer is offered:

"Eternal Father, I offer Thee the most Precious Blood of Thy Divine Son, Jesus, in union with the Masses said throughout the world today, for all the holy souls in Purgatory, for sinners everywhere, for sinners in the universal church, those in my own home and within my family. Amen."

St. Pio, in addition to his daily Mass, made about ten Spiritual Communions a day! That's how much he thought of Spiritual Communions! Many saints throughout the ages have been great advocates of spiritual communions including St. John Paul II and St. Teresa of Jesus (Teresa of Avila). Following is a prayer composed by St. Alphonsus Liguori:

"My Jesus, I believe that You are present in the most Blessed Sacrament. I love You above all things and I desire to receive You into my soul. Since I cannot now receive You sacramentally, come at least spiritually into my heart. I embrace You as if You have already come and unite myself wholly to You. Never permit me to be separated from You. Amen."

"All the good works in the world are not equal to the Holy Sacrifice of the Mass because they are the works of men; but the Mass is the work of God. Martyrdom is nothing in comparison, for it is but the sacrifice of man to God; but the Mass is the sacrifice of God for man." (St. John Vianney, the Cure d'Ar)

LED BY THE SPIRIT

A number of years ago I decided to pray the novena prayers to the Holy Spirit to ask the Holy Spirit to help me become a more loving child of God, a more loving wife, mother, and neighbor. I don't expect God to answer my prayers immediately, and so I continued to pray the novena prayers every day for quite some time. Eventually my husband and I were introduced to information about the Marriage Encounter weekend. It is recommended for couples with good marriages to make them even better marriages, and Ed and I decided to go. It is given by a priest and also facilitated by two or three couples.

The open sharing by these other couples helped Ed and I along with the other couples present, to share more deeply with each other later, in the privacy of our rooms. It turned out to be a wonderful weekend for us. ("Retrovaille," or the "Rediscovery" weekend is the one recommended for troubled marriages).

The Marriage Encounter movement was begun by Father Gabriel Calvo, in Spain, in 1958. It reached the United States in 1966 when

Father Calvo and Father Donald Hessler began presenting Marriage Encounters to Spanish speaking couples in New York, New Jersey, Illinois, Texas, Michigan and Ohio. At the Christian Family Movement convention at Notre Dame in 1967, the Encounter was given in Spanish and translated into English to eight couples and six priests who then decided to stay and sign up for it. It made a big hit, and English-speaking Marriage Encounter Weekends began.

Ed and I were married for 18 years when we went on the Marriage Encounter Weekend. We found it to be a great experience! Soon after, we were invited to join with other couples and a priest who had made a Marriage Encounter weekend. We met once a month in each other's homes and it was a wonderful group of people. And, because we had a priest present, we were able to have Mass in the home. For this blessing we were all very grateful.

The sharing of the couples and the priest helped all of us to grow in our love for Our Lord and for each other. In addition to praying grace before dinner as a family, which we had done since we were first married, my husband and I started praying together every evening before retiring, because of the sharing of one of the couples. This eventually led to praying the Rosary together.

THE POWER OF THE ROSARY

How difficult it seemed to me, years ago, to pray the Rosary. I found it hard to keep my mind on it, but I knew that our Blessed Mother Mary was asking us to pray the Rosary daily when at Fatima, Portugal in 1917 she visited three children, Lucia, Jacinta and Francesco and requested that they tell the people, "Pray the Rosary." And so, I just kept praying for the grace.

When I received Holy Communion at Mass I would ask the Blessed Mother to visit my heart to help me prepare to receive Our Lord. I begged her to forgive me for not praying the Rosary and I would ask her to grant me the grace to say it. I also asked St. Joseph, all the angels, and all the saints to visit me also, (a little hint I received from reading the autobiography of St. Thérèse).

Well, eventually I received that grace; and now, not only have I been able to pray the Rosary for many years every day (with the help of the grace Our Lady obtained for me), my husband and I have been instrumental in others taking up the practice. One of my good friends gave me a small, hard covered booklet entitled, "Scriptural

Rosary" and I found it a tremendous help in keeping my mind on the mysteries of the Rosary because this booklet had a line of scripture for each "Hail Mary." Our pastor gave us his permission to place some hand-made, blessed rosaries in baskets along with leaflets on how to pray the rosary. We also included bookmark-type cards with the wonderful promises of Our Lady that were given to St. Dominic and Blessed Alan for all of those who pray it.

One day, after Mass, a woman came up to me and asked, "Are you the wonderful woman who puts the rosaries out?" "I'm not so wonderful," I told her, "but, yes, I do." All of a sudden, tears welled up in her eyes and she told me how happy she was to have picked up one of the rosaries. She used to pray the Rosary every day years ago but then she got away from it and she told me that now she is saying it again. She was so grateful for this gift provided, and I was so thankful she shared that with me.

Even so, sometime later, I found myself thinking, "Am I some nut, putting out sacramentals?" Besides the rosaries, with the pastor's permission, we also put out leaflets explaining the Divine Mercy devotion given especially for our times by Our Lord to St. Maria

Faustina, along with blessed scapulars and other similar religious items as well. Within two or three days after this thought entered my mind, I went to adoration at a neighboring church that had 24-hour adoration of the Blessed Sacrament, five days a week. Soon after I came into the chapel I noticed a man, sitting diagonally across from me, praying with a pink rosary like the ones we have in the baskets in our church. I looked to see if there was a Miraculous Medal attached to it and I could see there was! We always attach the Miraculous Medals onto the rosaries when we get them. Right then, I knew this was a confirmation from Our Lord that it was okay to continue in this apostolate.

"Love the Madonna and pray the Rosary, for her Rosary is the weapon against the evil of the world today." (Saint Pio of Pietrelcina)

~~~~~~~

My mother and stepfather, Frank Droesch, bought a mobile home in Florida after they retired. They lived there from October to June each year and then would travel back up North for the summer. While they were down

South, my stepfather had a stroke which left his right arm and hand paralyzed. Although they had a home-health aide coming in two or three times a week, my mother found the care of Dad very difficult. Whenever I called her on the telephone I would hear her tales of woe and she sounded so very down. After a while I found it difficult calling her because the sadness in her voice was getting depressing, but I forced myself to phone her out of my love for the two of them.

One day after her usual complaints, I suggested that she offer her difficulties as part of her purgatory and she answered so humbly, "I never thought of that." I decided to send her a Rosary blessed by Pope Paul VI. A few weeks later when she answered the telephone, I was shocked to hear a big change in her voice. She actually sounded cheerful! I was so happy to hear such a difference in her attitude.

After we talked awhile she confided to me that she had started to pray the Rosary using the one I had sent her. "Since I've been praying the rosary," she told me, "I feel better now." How happy I was that I sent it to her, and how grateful I was, and am even now, to our Blessed Mother for the graces she obtained for my mother, who was then able to accept my stepfather's disability with a lot more patience and peace.

~~~~~~~~~

A few years ago, we had our grandchildren Marianne and Rosie for the weekend. It was during the winter and the weather was quite cold. We were getting ready to go to Sunday Mass when I noticed that Rosie did not have her undershirt on under her dress. I was afraid she'd be awfully cold so I told her to go and put her undershirt on. Rosie was five years old at the time, and she was always smiling unless you crossed her, and so on this particular day, she was not happy about having to get redressed. I could hear her complaining to her sister from the other room until I finally had to give in so we wouldn't be late for Mass. "Okay Rosie," I said, "Just put a sweater on under your coat and it will be all right." So off we went to Mass but Rosie could not seem to get out of her mood. She was very cranky and her sister tried to console her.

Whenever I bring any of the grandchildren to Mass with me I always bring a few religious books written for children, and I offer them one at a time to keep them prayerfully occupied during the Mass. The books I pick always have lots of lovely religious pictures. Rosie always enjoyed reading these books when she was with me at church, but this time she would have none of them.

Finally I searched my purse and found two rosaries and offered them to the girls. They were both very happy to accept them. All of a sudden I saw Rosie holding up her rosary with much attention to it and I wondered, "Could she be praying the Rosary?" After a while, she handed it back to me and said, "I feel better now." These were the exact words her great grandmother, my mother, when she lived in Florida, said to me after she started praying the Rosary I sent her.

During the rest of the Mass, and for the rest of the day, Rosie was her usual happy, smiling self. Praise God, and thank you Blessed Mother!

When I told my daughter Mary what happened, she told me that every day in the Catholic school that Rosie and Marianne attended, a decade of the Rosary is prayed over the loudspeaker and the children join in. Therefore Rosie was quite familiar with praying the Rosary.

My friend Laura has a daughter Amy who had plans to go out with her friends one evening, and Amy was going to be the driver. Laura asked her daughter to call her when she arrived at her destination. It was raining heavily and as the evening progressed, Laura had a very unusual feeling of foreboding come over her. She took out her rosary, and started praying one Rosary after another until she heard from her daughter. Finally the phone rang! Laura's daughter told her that she and her friends were in an accident, but everything was okay. Nobody was hurt.

It seems they were driving on a highway when bright headlights in the rear view mirror blinded Amy, and she began to drive onto the grassy shoulder of the highway. The front seat passenger grabbed the wheel, causing Amy to lose control of the car and go across two lanes of the highway and down an embankment into a dense grove of trees. Amy was able to stop the car, barely missing hitting a tree!

A state trooper had seen the accident, and when he arrived at the scene, he couldn't believe his eyes! He never saw anything like it! The car did not have a scratch on it, even though the trees were very close to the car on either side. The car had to be pushed out from between trees before they could even open the front doors. The troopers said that at the speed they were traveling, if they had hit one of those trees, everyone in the car probably would have been killed. Laura knew the reason why the five occupants of the car had escaped that outcome - her prayers that evening for their safety were answered. How thankful Laura was to our Blessed Mother for taking such good care of her daughter and her friends.

"For you make me glad, O LORD, by your deeds; at the works of your hands I rejoice."
(Psalm 92:5)

The founder of the Marian Movement of Priests, Fr. Stefano Gobbi, after visiting Fatima, Portugal in 1975 and praying to Our Lady about his concerns in the Church, received an inner locution from her to start the Marian Movement. During one of the cenacles which Fr. Gobbi held in the United States, he was urged by many to ask Our lady specifically what could be done to save the youth from the seductions of the world which were leading many of them astray and causing them to leave the Church. Our Lady gave Fr. Gobbi this definite and final solution to console the parents who are so concerned about the salvation of their children: Pray the Rosary! Every time you pray the Rosary say: "With this Rosary I bind all my children to the Immaculate Heart of Mary." In doing so, Our Lady promised "to see to their souls."

When my husband and I pray the Rosary we bind our children and all our family, friends and neighbors to the Immaculate Heart of Mary. (We don't think our Blessed Mother minds this addition). At our Cenacle prayer group we all do the same.

The Marian Movement of Priests is spread throughout the world and has Bishops, priests, religious and lay people included in its membership in response to our Blessed Mother's request to multiply the Cenacles of prayer.

For more information:
mmp@mmp-usa.net or call 207-398-3375.

Bishop Fulton J. Sheen was once asked to describe the power of the Rosary. His answer was, "There are no *words* to describe the power of the Rosary."

Sister Lucia, a Carmelite nun, died at the age of 97. She was one of the three children who were visited by Our Blessed Mother at Fatima, Portugal in 1917. In an interview with Fr. Augustin Fuentes in 1957, who was the postulator of the cause in the beatification of Jacinta & Francisco Marto, Sr. Lucia said:

"The Most Holy Virgin, in these last times in which we live, has given a new efficacy to the recitation of the Rosary to such an extent that there is no problem, no matter how difficult it is, temporal or especially spiritual, in the personal life of each one of us, of our families, of the families of the world or of the religious communities, or even of the life of peoples or nations, that cannot be solved by the Rosary. There is no problem I tell you, no matter how difficult it is, that we cannot resolve by the prayer of the Holy Rosary. With the Holy Rosary we will save ourselves. We will sanctify ourselves. We will console Our Lord and obtain the salvation of many souls."

Jacinta & Francisco Marto who died at the

early ages of 9 and 10 years old respectively were canonized saints by Pope Francis on May 13, 2017.

The Fifteen Promises of Mary to Christians Who Recite the Rosary:

1. *Whoever shall faithfully serve me by the recitation of the Rosary shall receive signal graces.*
2. *I promise my special protection and the greatest graces to all those who shall recite the Rosary.*
3. *The Rosary shall be a powerful armor against hell; it will destroy vice, decrease sin and defeat heresies.*
4. *It will cause virtue and good works to flourish; it will obtain for souls the abundant mercy of God; it will withdraw the hearts of men from the love of the world and its vanities and will lift them to the desire of eternal things. Oh, that souls would sanctify themselves by this means!*
5. *The soul which recommends itself to me by the recitation of the Rosary will not perish.*
6. *Whoever shall recite the Rosary devoutly,*

applying himself to the consideration of the sacred mysteries, shall never be conquered by misfortune. God will not chastise him in His justice; he shall not perish by an unprovided death; if he be just, he shall remain in the grace of God and become worthy of eternal life.

7. *Whoever shall have a true devotion for the Rosary shall not die without the sacraments of the Church.*

8. *Those who are faithful to recite the Rosary shall have during their life and at their death the light of God and the plentitude of His graces; at the moment of death they shall participate in the merits of the saints in Paradise.*

9. *I shall deliver from Purgatory those who have been devoted to the Rosary.*

10. *The faithful children of the Rosary shall merit a high degree of merit in Heaven.*

11. *You shall obtain all you ask of me by the recitation of the Rosary.*

12. *All those who propagate the Holy Rosary shall be aided by me in their necessities.*

13. *I have obtained from my Divine Son that all the advocates of the Rosary shall have for intercessors the entire celestial court*

during their life and at the hour of death.

14. *All who recite the Rosary are my sons, and brothers of my only Son, Jesus Christ.*

15. *Devotion to my Rosary is a great sign of predestination.*

(Given to St. Dominic and Blessed Alan de la Roche) Imprimatur: + Patrick J. Hayes, D.D., Archbishop of New York

Note: A plenary indulgence may be gained for ourselves or a soul in purgatory when the Rosary is recited in a church, a public oratory, a family group, a religious community, or a pious association. A partial indulgence is granted for its recitation in all other circumstances. (The usual conditions for gaining a plenary indulgence apply. In order to gain an indulgence one must be in the state of grace at least at the time the indulgenced work is completed.)

Further information: A leaflet (PR2), in Spanish (PRS), illustrating, in color, the mysteries of the Rosary with instructions on how to pray this devotion, may be obtained from the Marians of the Immaculate Conception, 1-800-462-7426 or ShopMercy.org

Anyone interested in the helpful Scriptural Rosary book, published by Christianica, may obtain one from the Marians listed above, or the Daughters of St. Paul at www.pauline.org, or by telephone 212-754-1110.

EWTN (The Eternal Word Television Network) broadcasts the Rosary in the Holy Land on Monday through Friday at 7:30 a.m., EST and on Saturday and Sunday from Lourdes at that time. The Rosary is also broadcast at other times during the day and evening. The Chaplet of the Divine Mercy is on every day on EWTN at 3:00 p.m.

A free CD of The Rosary and Divine Mercy Chaplet may be obtained from the Mary Foundation at www.catholicity.com

A woman, after Mass one Sunday, said to me, "You see these CD's of the Rosary? I gave one to a few of my friends and now their *husbands* are praying the Rosary!!"

MY MOTHER'S DEATH

When my mother and stepfather were up north during the summer of 1978 she complained of a cough that just wouldn't go away. Later that fall she was hospitalized in order to have a biopsy done. While she was there as a patient, a Catholic priest, who was one of the hospital chaplains, visited her and administered the Sacrament of the Sick.

That same afternoon I went to see my mother and when I kissed her on the cheek I smelled a heavenly aroma and wondered about it. I thought, maybe one of the nurses put some talcum powder on her that had a lovely scent. Soon my mother told me about the priest's visit. When he anointed her with the holy oil, she smelled, as she put it, "A heavenly aroma!!"

"Mommy," I said, "I smelled it when I kissed you!" What a wonderful gift Our Lord gave my mother, and me also, by allowing us to experience the heavenly perfume.

When Mom came home from the hospital, she came to live with us while she was undergoing chemotherapy treatments. Our son Jack gladly gave up his bedroom for his Nana's comfort because it had a bathroom adjacent to it.

My husband Ed and I often said our Rosary at night with my Mom in her room. I could tell she looked forward to our praying together, and in fact I remember her asking, "Are we going to say the Rosary now?" But I always suggested that if she wasn't up to praying out loud she could just listen in her heart while we prayed.

Mom became too sick to come with us to Mass on Sundays – before her illness she and Dad always went to Mass together. With my mother's permission, I decided to ask one of our parish priests, Fr. Walsh, to come to our home to administer the sacraments to her. He gladly came, heard her confession (the Sacrament of Reconciliation), gave her Holy Communion, and administered the Sacrament of the Sick (which can be given more than once during a person's illness). Although we were hoping Mom would get better, as it turned out she was being well-prepared for her journey back home to Our Lord.

In December of that year, my mother grew much weaker and told us she thought she should go back to the hospital. Our daughter Diane gave her a pair of red socks for Christmas and Mom got quite a kick out of them. She enjoyed wearing them on Christmas Day, and loved showing them off to the nurses and the aides. Mom was such a good patient; she was a good example to all of us. In fact, the day the doctor told her she had lung cancer she told me, "I thought I had enough suffering in my life." (She had lost her baby boy, Robert, at the age of two months, and was widowed during the depression years when I was a year and a half and my sister, only five years old).

"But all right," she quickly added, and I could see she was accepting God's will with only a moment's hesitation.

My sister Dot took time off from her business every other day to visit with Mom. She also had her brother and sisters popping in on her to keep her company. The day before she died my sister and I were with our Mother. We both knew she didn't look good. I had a small crucifix with me and I told my mom I would like her to gain a plenary indulgence for herself (complete remission of all the temporal punishment due to sin). I showed her the crucifix and asked her to say, "My Jesus Mercy," which she did. Before I left the hospital, I placed a blessed scapular on my Mother's pillow.

When I went home I called her sister Margie who lived near the hospital and asked her to visit my mother that evening. Although she had just washed her hair, she quickly dried it and went right over. Soon I received a phone call from Margie who was at the hospital with two of her other sisters, Betty and Marie.

"Jackie," Margie said, "Your mother is calling for you." I told Margie that when I was there earlier I had prayed with my mother, and Margie answered, "Maybe that's what she wants, for us to pray." She told me later that the three sisters began to pray the Rosary and after each decade my mother would say, "More." They kept on saying decade after decade because my mother kept saying, "more," until finally Betty began the "Hail Holy Queen." My mother gave them a big smile when they finished. She died the next morning.

When the doctor called me to tell me the sad news I asked him, "Why didn't you tell me death was so close." He answered, "I thought you knew." Because I was on my way out to Mass, I decided I could do more good for my mother by offering my Mass for her rather than going to the hospital since she had already passed away. I found out later that her sister Loretta arrived at the hospital from Long Island soon after her death and was allowed by the nurses to go in and visit my mother before she was taken away. The nurses told my aunt that they were with my mother when she died and were praying for her. How beautiful! God bless those nurses!

When I arrived at Immaculate Conception Church I noticed my next-door neighbor Carol McCarthy was there to attend Mass. I told her that my mother passed away that very morning and asked her to pray for her. When Fr. Walsh came out to offer the Mass, I went up and quietly told him the news and asked him to remember my mother in his prayers. To my wonderful surprise, he stepped forward and announced to the congregation that, "Jackie's mother passed away this morning," and asked everyone to remember her in their prayers.

How grateful I was that I made the decision to go to Church rather than to the hospital, knowing that much more was gained for my mother that way.

Many relatives and friends made the effort to be with us at my mother's wake. When we said our last goodbyes at the funeral parlor before they closed the casket, I left the room to get my stole and started to cry. The funeral director helped me put it on, and as he covered my shoulders with it, I smelled a heavenly aroma. Immediately my tears left me and a great consolation filled me.

Our friend, Fr. John J. Leonard, S.J., offered a beautiful Mass of the Resurrection on the day of her burial. During his homily he mentioned how my mother kept saying, "More" as her sisters prayed the Rosary decades around her bedside the night before she died.

At my mother's gravesite, etched on her tombstone, we have a rose and two of the symbols that are on the back of the Miraculous Medal: a Cross and attached to the Cross by a bar, the letter M: "To Jesus through Mary."

THE BROWN SCAPULAR OF
OUR LADY OF MOUNT CARMEL

About 20 years ago I was at Immaculate Conception Parish in Tuckahoe, N.Y. for the weekday Mass at 12:00 p.m. I noticed a young couple there whom I had never seen before. The young fellow had blonde, shoulder length hair and the girl he was with seemed quite upset. After the Mass I couldn't help notice that she was crying and he was trying to console her. They stayed for a while after Mass to pray and it was obvious to me that they were especially praying to our Blessed Mother Mary to ask her to intercede with her Divine Son for them. I just *had* to go up to them and offer some help, even though it was with much trepidation, not knowing how they would react.

I looked into my purse and decided to give them a blessed Brown Scapular of Our Lady of Mt. Carmel. I didn't know how they would accept it, they were a lot younger than I, but I just had to do something! I gently approached them and said, "You're praying to the right one," and I offered them the blessed scapular. I didn't want to pry, so I didn't ask them what was the matter. They gratefully accepted the scapular, thanked me so much, and left church soon after that.

The next day when I went to Mass, they were also there. After the Mass, the young fellow came up to me and again thanked me wholeheartedly. "Things are so much better now," he said! I was so happy for them, but I told him, "Don't thank me, thank the Blessed Mother!" I then went up to the Blessed Mother's altar and thanked her personally. All of a sudden, a woman approached me and asked, "Are you the woman who gave my son the Brown Scapular?" When I told her yes; she thanked me so very much and was visibly filled with emotion. I told her, as I told the young man, "Don't thank me, thank the Blessed Mother." She looked up at the shrine to Our Lady to silently offer a prayer of thanks-giving and started to leave, but then she stopped and asked me, "Do you know what the problem was?" I said, "No." She told me her other son was on a motorcycle and a truck ran over him *and* the cycle. He was in the hospital in a coma. They put the Brown Scapular on him and he came out of the coma. "He woke up," she told me! How wonderful! Praise God and His most Blessed Mother for answering their prayers!

~~~~~~

At Aylesford, England, on July 16, 1251, during difficult times, Mary, the Mother of Our Lord Jesus, appeared to St. Simon Stock, the Superior General of the Carmelite Order who was praying fervently to her for help. She held in her hand the Scapular of Carmel and assured him, saying: ***"....Whosoever dies wearing this Scapular shall not suffer eternal fire."***

The Brown Scapular - promotes confidence in Mary's protection while she intercedes to assist us in our trials in this life and eventually to help us enter eternal life with God in Heaven. "Mary, the exalted Daughter of Sion, helps all her children, wherever they may be and whatever their condition, to find in Christ the path to the Father's house." ([St.] John Paul II, *Redemptoris Mater, 47).*

Any priest or deacon can bless the scapular. Anyone wanting to be enrolled in the Confraternity of the Scapular may be enrolled by any priest or deacon or a person authorized by the Carmelite Order. The scapular can also be replaced afterwards by a blessed Scapular Medal, which has on one side the image of the Sacred Heart of Jesus and on the other, the image of Mary. This concession was granted by Pope Pius X at the request of missionaries in the tropics where cloth scapulars quickly deteriorated and wearing them became uncomfortable. However, the wearing of the cloth scapular has always been highly recommended, especially in countries where the climate does not present similar difficulties. St. John Paul II, St. Pius X and St. Thérèse of Lisieux all wore the cloth scapular.

We are encouraged by the Carmelites to pray the Hail Mary, daily, three times to express our devotion to our Blessed Mother. (Hopefully, this will eventually lead to praying the Rosary, so often requested by Our Lady at her different apparition sites including Fatima and Medjugorje).

"One day through the Rosary and Scapular I will save the world."
(The Blessed Virgin Mary to Saint Dominic).

Note: Anyone wanting to purchase a Rosary or a Brown Scapular, or both, may order one from:

EWTN Religious Catalogue
www.ewtnreligiouscatalogue.com or call 1-800-

854-6316. Also available on DVD or CD is The Holy Rosary in The Holy Land, which is beautifully done.

YOUNG MAN ON THE HIGHWAY

Sometimes my husband and I attended what is called a Marriage Encounter Renewal evening. We had not been to one for quite some time when I heard about a renewal night that was being held farther north from where we lived. It meant taking the Sprain Brook Parkway to get there. I asked my husband if he would like to go and he agreed, but when the time came to leave, I noticed he had fallen asleep while he was sitting on the sofa in the living room. I wondered whether I should awaken him or let him sleep and forget about going. I decided to say a prayer to the Holy Spirit to guide me as to what to do. All of a sudden Eddie opened his eyes and was ready to go!

I can't remember anything about that Renewal evening other than what happened on the way home on the highway. As we were driving along, we could see in the distance some people waving cars over to the right hand lane. I thought there might be a deer lying on the highway. As we drew closer I saw it was a man that had been run over by a car. I asked my husband to pull over onto the grass, which he did. He stopped the car and we went to see if we could help. There was a taxicab parked on the grass, plus one other car with a young woman standing by crying hysterically. I walked over to the young man lying in the road who was obviously dead. Cars were speeding by me, and I admit to being a little afraid as people were calling out to me that I might be hit by another car. But I said to myself, "The Blessed Mother will protect me," and she did. I took a blessed brown scapular of Our Lady of Mount Carmel out of my purse and placed it on the forehead of the young man and prayed a Hail Mary out loud hoping he would hear me as the hearing is the last to go when we die. My husband came over and also blessed him with a very special relic.

All of a sudden the police were there and the officer said to me, "Lady, that man is dead." "I know," I said, "We're just praying for him." "Oh okay," he replied. Then we went over and spoke to the people and found out the whole story. The young man was a Catholic, as were his parents, so I went over to the police officer and asked him to call a priest, which he did. Soon the priest arrived and gave the young man conditional absolution of all his sins. Knowing God's mercy, a priest may give conditional absolution for the dying or those who have passed away because we are not certain when the soul separates from the body.

Our Lord Jesus revealed to Sister Faustina (now St. Faustina) that every soul receives a final grace at the last moment before death. "But-horror!-there are also souls who voluntarily and consciously reject and scorn this grace! Although a person is at the point of death, the merciful God gives the soul that interior vivid moment, so that if the soul is willing, it has the possibility of returning to God. But sometimes, the obduracy in souls is so great that consciously they choose hell; they [thus] make useless all the prayers that other souls offer to God for them and even the efforts of God Himself..."(*Diary*, 1698)

The young man's mother and uncle were there with the taxi cab driver. The mother had called the cab to bring her son to a hospital hoping that he would be admitted to the psychological unit because he was very much troubled. The hospital did not admit him but sent him home instead. On the way home there was an argument in the back seat of the cab and the cab driver pulled over to the side. The young man jumped out and ran across the highway right in front of a young woman's car, and she had no way of avoiding hitting him. The poor girl was so upset, as anyone could imagine.

The priest who came entered the cab with the mother and the uncle and tried to console them as best as he could. Of course we all stayed until an ambulance came and took the body away. My husband and I then drove the young woman home, as she was in no condition to drive a car. She was so grateful that we stopped to help and then drove her home. That poor thing was so shook up!

I looked in the newspaper the next day or so to see if there was any notice of the accident. I also looked in the obituaries and was amazed to read that the young man we had stopped to pray and get a priest for, was a member of our parish church! I always pray for all who are going to die during the week, especially our next relative, friend, neighbor or anyone in our parish for the grace of a holy death.

What a gift it was from the Holy Spirit that we happened to drive by right after the accident happened and were able to help a young man and his family from our very own parish!

THE DIVINE MERCY IMAGE

Anyone desiring to purchase this image may do so by contacting:

Mercy of the Lord Ministries, 395 Miller Street, Ludlow, MA 01056, 413-583-6830.

Jesus, The Divine Mercy

One day as I was leaving our church after the 12:00 p.m. Mass, one of the women who also attended daily Mass motioned me over to the book rack in the vestibule in the back of the church. She picked up one of the leaflets on the "Devotion to The Divine Mercy" which had a picture on the front of Jesus, pointing to His heart from which issued red and pale rays of light. At the bottom of the image were the words, "Jesus, I Trust in You!" She told me, "Ever since I picked up one of these leaflets some time ago, I've been praying the Chaplet of Mercy that's inside the leaflet every day." How wonderful! She was also there for the recitation of the Rosary every weekday before the noon Mass.

Inside the "The Devotion to The Divine Mercy" (MPL2) leaflet, (in Spanish, SMDS2), which can be obtained from the Marian Press in Stockbridge, Massachusetts, it tells of Our Lord's revelations in the 1930s to a young religious, Sister Faustina, who was a member of the Congregation of the Sisters of Our Lady of Mercy, in Krakow, Poland. Our Lord Jesus wants the whole world to know of His infinite mercy.

The following quotes are taken from her diary. He told Sister Faustina, *"I never reject a contrite heart."* (*Diary, 1485*). *"Sooner would heaven and earth turn into nothingness than would My mercy not embrace a trusting soul."* (*Diary, 1777*). He also said, *"...I am Love and Mercy itself."* (*Diary, 1074*) *"Let no soul fear to draw near to Me, even though its sins be as scarlet."* (*Diary, 699*). *"The greater the sinner, the greater the right he has to My mercy."* (*Diary, 723*).

Jesus taught her to pray the "Chaplet of Mercy" on ordinary rosary beads. It's a powerful, simple prayer calling on God's mercy for ourselves and for the whole world. Our Lord told Sister, *"...Whoever will recite it (the Chaplet) will receive great mercy at the hour of death.... Even if there were a sinner most hardened, if he were to recite this chaplet only once, he would receive grace from My infinite mercy. I desire that the whole world know My infinite mercy. I desire to grant unimaginable graces to those souls who trust in My mercy."* (*Diary, 687; see also 1541*).

The Chaplet is prayed on ordinary rosary beads and begins with the Our Father, the Hail Mary, and the Apostles Creed.

Then, on the Our Father beads we pray:

"Eternal Father, I offer You the Body and Blood, Soul and Divinity of Your dearly beloved Son, Our Lord Jesus Christ, in atonement for our sins and those of the whole world."

On the Hail Mary beads we pray:

"For the sake of His sorrowful Passion, have mercy on us and on the whole world."

In conclusion we pray three times:

"Holy God, Holy Mighty One, Holy Immortal One, have mercy on us and on the whole world." (Diary 476)

This efficacious chaplet takes only about seven minutes to pray, or a mere 10 minutes if you pray slowly. What a wonderful gift from Our Lord! Sister Faustina wrote, "...I heard these words: *'At the hour of their death, I defend as My own glory every soul that will say this chaplet; or when others say it for a dying person..."* (*Diary,* 811). She understood how important it is to pray the Chaplet of Mercy for the dying. She wrote, "Oh, if only everyone realized how great the Lord's mercy is and how much we all need that mercy, especially at that crucial hour!"

There is a pamphlet "The Divine Mercy Novena and Chaplet," LFMCN which is available from the Marians that contain the Novena and Chaplet. Other revelations of Our Lord to Sister Faustina for the benefit of souls are explained in the MPL2 leaflet, such as: Divine Mercy Sunday, the Hour of Great Mercy and the Image of The Divine Mercy. Jesus told Sister Faustina that, "Not only are we to **receive** His mercy, but we are to use it, being merciful to others by our actions, by our words, and by our prayers...."

"Sister Faustina's spiritual life was based on deep humility, purity of intention, and loving obedience to the will of God in imitation of the virtues of the Blessed Virgin Mary. Her special devotion to Mary Immaculate and to the sacraments of Eucharist and Reconciliation [Confession] gave her the strength to bear all her sufferings as an offering to God on behalf of the Church and those in special need, especially great sinners and the dying." *(Quote from the booklet M17, "The Divine Mercy Message and Devotion.")*

Sister Faustina was canonized a saint by Pope John Paul II on April 30, 2000, the first saint of the new Millennium.

"If we say, "We are without sin," we deceive ourselves, and the truth is not in us. If we acknowledge our sins, he is faithful and just and will forgive our sins and cleanse us from every wrongdoing."
(1 John 1:8-9)

BILL'S CONVERSION STORY

Bill had heard of Our Lady's protection, and willingly shares his story which follows.

Our Lady protects the weak like any mother who nurtures and teaches her children. Our Lady's protective care of me shows that Our Lord truly gave her to be our mother as He was dying on the cross.

I am a "cradle Catholic" who had a devotion to Our Lady when I was only seven or eight years old. I recall finding a statue of Our Lady as a child and assembling a small area in which I could venerate her. At a much earlier time, when I was about four years old, my mother took me to the doctor because my parents found me at the window at night having a conversation with someone while looking at the moon. My mother says I called the person "Nini." The doctor laughed and said I was saner than my parents. To this day, I wonder if I was speaking to Our Lady and whether "Nini" was a child's effort to say "Mary."

Of course, time went on and I grew up in the 1960s and 1970s: an easy time to lose devotion to Our Lord and Our Lady. I stopped attending Mass after college graduation in 1980; thinking why did an educated person need to go to church? I'm ashamed to think back on my activities in college and wonder how I had the nerve to receive Holy Communion without first making a good confession and amending my Bohemian ways!! (It is a sacrilege to receive Holy Communion when not in the state of grace, that is, free of mortal [serious] sin).

Then, I went on to law school and graduate business school so that, by the early 1990s, I was scoffing at the Church and making passing jokes about Our Lady. Our Lord and Our Lady had other plans for my life and they intervened when I least expected it.

In 1995, I resigned abruptly from my job because I suspected wrongdoing was taking place at my employer's offices. I had no job prospects and could not tell people why I left because I would be violating a client's confidences. When the news came out about what was happening, even though I had done the right thing, I was painted with a "broad brushstroke" and could not get a job in the same industry; it was guilt by association.

The Lord protected me and had plans to alter my life. With plenty of time on my hands,

I turned to EWTN (Eternal Word Television Network) and began to say the Rosary faithfully for the first time in my life. It was like a "conversation," the ability to speak with Heaven! Then, I began to recite the Chaplet of Divine Mercy. That too, was a strange and positive experience, because I was consciously praying for everyone, not just for myself! Nine months later, the Lord gave me a temporary opportunity that turned into a full-time job in a new industry. What a blessing!

The best is yet to come. The weekend following Thanksgiving, 1996 was the eve of the First Sunday of Advent, and relatives were visiting who wanted to attend the Vigil Mass. The Rosary, The Divine Mercy Chaplet and EWTN stirred up my conscience enough to know that I could not receive Holy Communion without making a good confession. So, I went to confession for the first time since my First Communion thirty years earlier!

I knelt in the Reconciliation Room and began to give my general confession. The priest asked: "What brought you back here?" As I told him, I could feel the presence of Our Lord next to me, standing by my side. I felt a warmth in my heart that radiated throughout my body. I started to cry. After the words of absolution, I did my penance and I remember it felt like I was floating, not walking out of the church, because when I came out of the confessional I knew Our Lord had forgiven me. I attended Mass that evening and received Our Lord for the first time in sixteen years. I will never leave the Church again.

There is no doubt that Our Lady continued to assist me during those lost years and eventually won me over and brought me back to her Son. She can touch a soul that is so hardened and guilty that it desires only to run from Our Lord out of fear! Never doubt the loving power of Our Lady and of her Rosary. Never doubt the power of Divine Mercy to bring back a soul.

As Our Lady continued to protect and guide me it became clear that my return to the Church in 1996 was not the last time that Our Lord was going to "work on my soul." Of course, He sent his Mother to me for guidance.

I was extremely grateful for my new job in a new industry. However, it meant that I started at the "bottom" rung on the salary ladder and the period of unemployment also added financial burdens. By early 2005, I was bankrupt. The Lord used this period to attack my pride and make me understand that, in all things, He is present to help me learn important lessons and to make me realize that I need Him in good times and in bad.

A family crisis also came to a head in 2005. My nieces and nephews whom I helped to raise were being taken to a nearby state to live with their mother after a bitter divorce. It seemed like the end of the world to lose contact with the children on a regular basis. Just days before the family court hearing that granted the mother's request to take the children to another state, Our Lady appeared at our parish church in Brookfield, Connecticut, when Vicka, one of the Medjugorje seers, had a public apparition of Our Lady during a church talk. One of Our Lady's comments to Vicka was striking and prophetic; the devil is attacking families and trying to destroy them. Clearly, the family court proceedings took on new meaning after Our Lady's comment about families under attack.

I felt like I was under attack as well. I turned to prayer. Certainly, it was not very fruitful prayer because I was fearful. Fear is a lack of trust in the Lord. Trust, as we know, is faith projected into the future. With fear in my heart, I attended Eucharistic Adoration from midnight to 1:00 a.m. At 12:36 a.m., alone in the Chapel, I heard a woman's voice from behind me say, "Why didn't you call me?" Startled, I looked around to see who had entered the Chapel without my knowledge. There was no one there. The woman's voice was not familiar, and it was not a phrase that I used. Then I realized that I called my mom each night at 7:00 p.m. to see whether she was all right and to check on my dad's condition. He was in a nursing home after a major stroke and the discovery that he had lung cancer. Then I went back to the voice. The woman's voice was not angry or emotional. It was calm and even-toned. And it was a young woman's voice. It became very clear that it was Our Lady reminding me that I should confide in her each day in prayer just as faithfully as I called my earthly mother each day.

Later that year, at the end of the summer, I went to Medjugorje for the first time. The spiritual blessings that one receives there cannot be described in words. In times of trouble, just thinking about attending outdoor Adoration at the back of St. James Church or of sitting at the Blue Cross near Apparition Hill, can bring peace to my soul years later. Our Lord and Our Lady granted me a special present in Medjugorje to let me know they are with me. One night we attended Ivan's public apparition at the Blue Cross. On the way back to our rooms, we walked through the dark vineyards toward town. As we turned a corner, we heard people ahead of us say, "Keep quiet and look up." There I saw a large ball of stars revolving in the sky near Cross Mountain. Three angels were revolving around the ball of stars in the opposite direction. People in the distance were laughing, singing, crying and praising the Lord. By my estimate based on the crowd's exclamations, there were about 50-100 people in the vineyard watching this miracle in the sky. My "earthly" mind made me wonder if this was a laser light show. No sooner had I finished the thought than a bolt of lightning came from the ball of stars and hit the ground. With that, I hit the ground on my knees. Laser light shows don't have bolts of lightning. In addition, there were no "tracer lights" or beams of light from the ground that laser lights produce. A second bolt of lightning came from the ball of stars and then a third bolt, and then the entire apparition disappeared. The cheering and cries from the crowd in the vineyard matched the feelings in my soul. What a great gift to sinners from their loving God!

Now, I have two Marian teachings to guide me: "Do whatever He tells you," "Why didn't you call me?" and from the pilgrims at Medjugorje, "Keep quiet and look up."

"I was hard pressed and was falling, / but the LORD helped me. My strength and my courage is the LORD, and he has been my savior."
(Psalm 118:13-14)

ANOTHER STORY OF DIVINE MERCY

When Ed and I owned a time-share in Florida, we met a couple when we went out for dinner one night. Let's call them Lee and Dave. We happened to be sitting at a table adjacent to theirs and at one point the four of us started up a conversation. It was as if we were friends for quite some time that's how easily we conversed with them. Lee told me this was her second marriage. She was a Catholic and Dave was of another Christian faith but the two of them went to Mass on Sundays and Holy Days, however she didn't receive Holy Communion because they weren't married in the Church. I think I may have given her a Green Scapular, but I do remember vividly giving Dave a leaflet on the Divine Mercy which he graciously accepted and put in his shirt pocket. We kept in touch with them and got together at times when we were in Florida. One day Lee told me that Dave had passed away but before he died, while he was in the hospital, he became a Catholic and received the sacraments. Lee went to Confession, (the Sacrament of Reconciliation) and was back to receiving Holy Communion at Mass. Praise God and His infinite mercy!

THE MOST BLESSED SACRAMENT

When we owned a summer place in the Catskills near Monticello, our parish church, St. Thomas Aquinas in Forestburgh, (New York), had Adoration of the Blessed Sacrament every first Friday for twenty-four hours. My husband and I gladly signed up to be with Our Lord for one of those hours each month. I took one of the daytime hours and Ed always signed up for the 2:00 a.m. to 3:00 a.m. shift. He always brought his Rosary and also a religious book along with him so he could do some spiritual reading.

This one particular night he forgot his glasses, so after he had prayed his Rosary he couldn't go on to his spiritual reading as usual, and his back was killing him. He was very frustrated until all of a sudden he heard within himself, "Just be with Me," in a voice he never heard before, and he knew it was Our Lord speaking to him. He was very much comforted!

Three o'clock came and went. The next scheduled adorer was supposed to arrive at that time but didn't. Ed knew he had to stay another hour even though his back was hurting. He felt like lying down in the pew but just couldn't do that when he thought about the suffering Our

Lord endured on the Cross. Four o'clock came and went. The adorer scheduled for 4:00 a.m. never showed!

In the meantime I woke up, noticed the time, and started to worry. If Ed isn't home by 5:15 a.m. I thought, I'll call our Deacon who didn't live too far from the church to ask him to go and see what happened. I thought Ed might have hit a deer on the way home which unfortunately did happen on occasion in our area. But Ed came home at 5:15 furious, first because his back was hurting so much and second because no one had come to fulfill his hour. He eventually found out that the fellow who signed up for the 3:00 a.m. and 4:00 a.m. hours, thought he was signing up for the afternoon hours. Anyhow, Ed went to bed exhausted! The next morning when he woke up, much to his surprise, all his back pain was gone! Praise God!

~~~~~~~

During the summer after I finished the sixth grade, my Aunt Evelyn and Uncle Dave invited me to spend a week at their lovely home in Teaneck, New Jersey. They were so good to me. My aunt invited a couple of girls my age in the neighborhood to meet me who helped so much to make my stay very enjoyable. I still have pictures of the three of us swimming in the lake that my aunt brought us to.

On Sunday I went to the local Catholic Church with one or both of the girls for Mass. (My aunt and uncle were not Catholic; they were Protestant as was my father before he converted, shortly before he married my mother). I assume it was announced at that time that one day during the week there was going to be a special service which included Benediction of the Blessed Sacrament. I remember being asked by one of the girls if I would like to go. I agreed, and when the time came during the week, off we went to be present at Church.

I still remember that when the priest blessed the people with the monstrance containing the Holy Eucharist, I was taken aback by the holy warmth of the rays coming to me from the Sacred Host. I thought to myself something like, "I could be a saint." Of course, eventually I came to understand that it wasn't anything I did personally that gave me this experience. It was Our Lord giving me a special blessing. Many years later I heard a priest say that ordinarily we don't feel the presence of God although He's always there. When He allows us to feel His presence (or His grace), it is an extra gift from Him.

It is only in recent years, that another priest instructed the people as to why before Benediction of the Blessed Sacrament a priest or deacon places a long, wide fringed scarf, called a humeral veil, over his shoulders, arms, and hands before he raises the monstrance to bless the people in the Sign of the Cross. He told us he covers himself and his hands because it is Jesus who is blessing the people, not the priest. And what a blessing it is, to be blessed by Jesus Himself! I have been to healing services where the priest has blessed the people with the Holy Eucharist in this way and how wonderful it was to be there!

It has been documented that most of the miracles that take place in Lourdes, France, have occurred during the blessing of the sick with the monstrance containing Our Lord Jesus in the Holy Eucharist.

Our friend Father Breault told us of what happened years ago when he was in Lourdes. Father officiated at the blessing of the sick one day. Afterwards a man came up to him and told him how he had experienced a special healing and thanked him for it. Father told him that he didn't do anything special; he just "slowed down a little bit" as he was blessing him with Our Lord.

THE POWER OF PRAYER

Many years ago I attended St. Nicholas of Tolentine Grammar and High School in the Bronx, New York from third through twelfth grade. For first and second grades I attended our previous parish of Our Savior, also in the Bronx. We were taught for the most part by the Dominican Sisters, with only a couple of lay teachers. I will be forever grateful to them for the love they instilled in us of Our Lord and His Blessed Mother and for the moral values they taught us. A close friend of mine, Janet, shared with me how grateful she is for all that the Sisters imparted to us. Thank God for those good Sisters!

When we were in the eighth grade, Sr. Mary Alacoque, O.P. shared with us that we all have doubts, at one time or another, about our faith. She recommended that when these doubts come, say, "Lord, I believe, help me to understand." I remembered and have since followed her advice all through my life. I can truthfully say that an inner light would often be given to me, maybe not immediately, I didn't expect that, but certainly eventually, for which I was and am very grateful.

"I believed, and then I understood."
(St. Augustine)

~~~~~~~

For many years my friend Mary, a daily communicant, had prayed for the return of her father whom she dearly loved, to the practice of his faith and to the sacraments of the Church. One day, she received a call from her brother saying that their father had suffered a heart attack and been taken to a local hospital. Upon his arrival at the emergency room, the doctors and nurses did the best they could, but her father succumbed and passed away. The next morning, Mary went to Mass at 8:00 a.m. and prayed for the repose of the soul of her dad. When Mass was over, in her grief she decided to go to the sacristy to ask the priest who celebrated Mass to pray for her father who had just died.

"What was your father's name?" the priest asked. When Mary told him, the priest said that he had happened to be in the emergency room when efforts were made to save her father. He was able to anoint her father in his last moments and helped prepare him to meet Our Lord. She was amazed that this was the priest who said the Mass that she attended, and she was filled with joy! All her prayers were answered.

How grateful she was that she was inspired to go to the sacristy after Mass to ask this priest to pray for her father. If she hadn't, she would never have known that her father received the Last Rites of the Church, and the grace of a happy death, which had been her most fervent hope.

~~~~~~~~

I think it was in the early 1980s when Ed's father, Frank came down with a bad cough that just wouldn't go away. During one of our visits to him I realized how poorly he looked and it scared me. I thought he was on his way out. Ed's mother was also quite concerned.

After Mass one day I went up to the tabernacle and prayed before Our Lord. I begged Him to please make Ed's father better and to grant the gift of having Mom and Dad live to celebrate their 50th wedding anniversary.

Later that day, I went to see my in-laws. Ed's father told me he didn't know what happened, "But," he said, "there's been a change." He improved dramatically and soon he was up and about as usual. Thanks be to God!!

As the date of Mom and Dad's 50th anniversary approached and plans needed to be made, Mom asked me if I thought it would be all right for them to have a Mass. I told her I thought that it would bring them many graces. She decided to ask our friend, Fr. John J. Leonard, S.J. to celebrate the Mass on their special day. Before the Mass began, Ed's father went into the sacristy, made his confession, and received the Sacrament of Reconciliation in preparation to receive Our Lord in Holy Communion alongside his wife. What a wonderful celebration the whole day was! Following the Mass there was a great reception with family and friends at their club. We also had music and dancing. How heart-warming it was to see Mom and Dad dancing together on their 50th wedding anniversary!

~~~~~~~~~

Our friend and former pastor of St. Thomas Aquinas Church, Forestburgh, New York, Monsignor Robert J. McCabe, shared with us the following story.

Father's parents, Valentine, "Val," and Elizabeth Lillian, "Lil," McCabe were getting on in years, having celebrated their 47th wedding anniversary. Their physical and mental health had started to deteriorate, and Lil McCabe was hospitalized for a serious case of cellulitis of the leg, and at the same time Val was diagnosed with Alzheimer's. Soon after his mother was discharged from the hospital and admitted to Francis Schervier Nursing Home, Father suggested to his three brothers, John, Tom and Paul, that they give family and friends a big party in honor of their parents at their home in Scarsdale, New York, while his parents were still able to enjoy it. His brothers agreed and the date was set for Sunday, September 30, 1982. They were planning to have an outdoor party for about a hundred people. One sister-in-law said, "What if it rains?"

While the initial reactions to the suggestion that it might rain raised immediate questions and doubts, Fr. McCabe, realizing that the celebration they were planning was not for them, but was so well-deserved by their parents, decided to put it this way: "God wouldn't let it rain on their parade." His parents were such wonderful people, and their home wouldn't accommodate all the guests they planned to invite, so Father prayed and believed that God would want to bless them with a beautiful day, since the party was going to be held outdoors, without any overhead protection.

An excellent caterer was contacted. Tables and chairs were generously provided for the celebration by the parish. Father had to pick up a friend of the family, Sister Miriam James, S.C., at Mount St. Vincent campus in Riverdale, New York on the day of the party which was to commence at 1:00 p.m. Sister was Father's mother's best friend and also happened to be his and his three brother's eighth grade teacher at Immaculate Heart of Mary Grammar School. As he turned onto the Cross County Parkway in Yonkers on the way back to his parents' home, the sky looked so ominous and full of clouds which promised rain, that Father kept praying to the good Lord to hold back the rain and give his parents a beautiful day. He became so distracted with keeping his hands on the wheel and his eyes on the road while simultaneously talking to Sister James in the back seat of the car, that he hardly noticed the poor weather conditions had quickly vanished! Lo and behold, when he arrived in Scarsdale at his parents' home, the dark clouds had disappeared and the weather turned out to be gorgeous!

His parents had a wonderful time! There was a band, and a lot of singing and dancing. His father danced up a storm, and Father has pictures to prove it! It was a great celebration. After the guests, caterer and band left around 8:00 p.m., Father went around collecting and folding the chairs provided by the church, to be put away in the rack. As he folded the last chair and placed it in the rack, the heavens opened and the rain came down "in buckets." God had answered Fr. McCabe's and everyone's prayers for a perfect day—no rain showers, but showers of love instead.

After the party was over, Father's mother was returned to the nursing home (where his father was soon to follow). Father made some tea and asked his dad how he enjoyed the party. His father answered, "What party?" Fr. McCabe realized then, that because of his father's Alzheimer's condition, although his dad had a wonderful time at the party he unfortunately didn't remember any of it. Father decided to let it go, and responded, "Okay, Dad," and proceeded to sit down to enjoy their tea together.

I was truly edified by Father's loving response to his Dad. He didn't say, "Don't you remember dancing with Aunt Tillie and all your family and friends being here to celebrate with you and Mom, etc." He realized in his charity, that questioning his father like this could have saddened him. He implicitly knew that it didn't make sense to discuss it any further since his father had no recollection of the day.

When all is said and done, isn't making someone happy in the present moment more important, even if he or she doesn't remember it?

"Ask and it will be given to you; seek and you will find; knock and the door will be opened to you. For everyone who asks, receives; and the one seeks, finds; and to the one who knocks, the door will be opened."
(Matthew 7:7-8)

AMONG MARY'S GIFTS, THE GREEN SCAPULAR

In the 1840's, the Mother of Our Lord Jesus, through a number of apparitions to Sister Justine Bisqueyburu, a Daughter of Charity of St. Vincent de Paul, asked her to have a scapular made according to what she was being shown. This sacramental was twice approved by Pope Pius IX in 1863 and again in 1870, when he said, "Write to these good Sisters that I authorize them to make and distribute it." The scapular has a picture of Our Lady on the front of it, and on the back, there is a picture of her Immaculate Heart, pierced by a sword, with a Cross over it, and the prayer around her heart, "Immaculate Heart of Mary pray for us now, and at the hour of our death."

Sr. Justine understood interiorly that the scapular was a gift from God for the conversion of souls, especially those far away from the Lord, and that those who wore it, would obtain the grace of a happy death through the intercession of the Blessed Virgin. It can be worn, carried or placed in one's room. In the case of an unbeliever it can also be secretly hidden. Each day the prayer on the scapular should be prayed, by the person receiving it, or by the one who gives it.

It is important to have the scapular blessed by a priest or deacon. Many conversions and miraculous cures have been attributed through the devout use of the Green Scapular.

~~~~~~~

About 20 years ago we needed service on our GE refrigerator. When the serviceman came, we started to talk and he told me that his two-year old daughter needed an operation on her skull because it wasn't getting larger as it was supposed to and her brain was getting crowded. I offered him a blessed Green Scapular for his daughter which he gratefully accepted.

About six months later someone rang our door bell. I was on my way out and was going to let my husband answer the door but he asked me to get it.

I asked, "Who is it?" and then someone answered, "You gave me a medallion once." I was puzzled, but opened the door. Then I noticed a GE serviceman's insignia on his shirt and I realized that I must have given him a green scapular in the past, so I asked him, "Do you mean a *Green Scapular*?" "Yes", he told me. He was in the neighborhood at a service call up the street to repair an appliance and decided to stop by to tell me, "So many wonderful things have happened since you gave me that Green Scapular six months ago." Then I remembered what he had told me those months prior about his daughter. "How is your daughter?" I asked. "She's fine," he answered. "She didn't need the operation after all." How happy I was to hear that!

Then he told me he'd been lending the scapular to others and they too have been getting better. He lent it to his uncle who had cancer and now he's doing well he said. He lent it to a friend who had AIDS and was dying and he was better. "To tell you the truth," he said, "He's living it up." "I wouldn't say he's cured," I responded. "He's been given more time to come back to the Lord."

Then he proceeded to tell me of a most awful experience. He was in his car and his was the first car having stopped for a red light. Just as the light turned green an ash fell off the cigarette he was smoking. He looked down to see where the ash landed. The man in the car behind him got very impatient and quickly pulled out to pass him. Unfortunately the driver coming from the other direction ran through the red light and crashed into the car that had been behind him and the man was killed. How sad for the man and his family. May God rest his soul. We both felt our GE serviceman was especially protected by our Blessed Mother.

Since he was lending his scapular out, I gave him ten more that had been blessed and he went happily on his way.

~~~~~~~~

Our daughter Debbie and son-in-law Billy were married by a priest and a rabbi on July 11, 1981. On May 8, 1982, they welcomed their first son, Joseph. When Joseph was two years old we asked Debbie and Billy if they would take care of our dog, Brandy, a mastiff, while we were away on vacation. We were only gone for two days when we got a phone call from Debbie, telling us that Billy was in the hospital. Of course we offered to come home, but Debbie said to wait until they found out the lab results and knew what they were dealing with.

What happened was on Sunday morning Brandy swatted Billy in the face with her paw, and when he woke up on Monday morning, he noticed he was black and blue under his eye. He thought that the dog may have broken his nose, so they went to the emergency room at the local hospital where Billy asked for an x-ray. Because Billy's own mother had passed away from brain cancer when Billy was only a year and a half old, he was very conscious of being careful about his health. He told them he was feeling very tired lately and asked if they would give him a blood test. They agreed and when the blood test was done, they were shocked to see that his white blood cell count was down to 200. Normally, the white count range is 4,300 to 10,800! The doctor immediately admitted Billy, telling him that they would need to run more tests and that he should be out of the hospital in a few days. A bone marrow aspiration was taken on Tuesday which confirmed that Billy had acute lymphoblastic leukemia. Left untreated, the doctor remarked that soon other more serious symptoms would have brought him to the hospital.

When Debbie got home that night from the hospital, she was understandably extremely upset. When she went to bed, she told me she took out her rosary and started to pray. At one point, while she was praying through her tears, she felt our Blessed Mother's presence and was filled with immediate peace. Within herself she heard Our Lady telling her, "Everything is going to be all right." Debbie wanted to trust completely in Our Lady's words but still she wondered if she really heard her consoling message since she never had an experience like this before.

As soon as we heard of Billy's diagnosis we left for home to be with our daughter and son-in-law. With heavy hearts we went straight to the hospital to see Billy. When we arrived, Debbie was there in the room with him. We noticed a Green Scapular hanging from his bed rail, and after visiting for a while we went outside the room to talk with our daughter. After hearing the whole story about what happened, I asked her if she had asked Billy, who is Jewish, if it was all right with him to put the scapular on his bed. She told me that she had asked him and he had said yes. I was very pleased that he accepted Debbie's offer, and also that she requested his permission first. Billy wore the scapular around his neck for about two months until it broke, and then he kept it in his night table.

He was eventually transferred to Sloan-Kettering Cancer Center in New York City where he received treatment. Eventually after five years of checkups, the doctor at Sloan-Kettering told Billy he didn't have to come back anymore. "You have just as much of a chance of getting leukemia again as anyone else that has not had the disease," he told him. And that was over 25 years ago!

After all the chemotherapy he had, there was some doubt if they would ever be able to have any more children. God has blessed them with two more, Jeffrey and Kimberlee, much to everyone's joy.

~~~~~~~~

One of the members of our church told me her father was critically ill and in the hospital, whereupon I gave her one of the Green Scapulars to bring to her Dad. Sometime later I saw her at a church function and asked how her father was doing. She told me he had passed away and said, "Jackie, my father wasn't a very good Catholic. He was in intensive care for 45 days, but I couldn't bring him the scapular the morning after you gave it to me because I was working. My husband works nights, so he brought it to the hospital about eleven o'clock in the morning. Within forty-five minutes of my husband

arriving at the hospital, my dad passed away."
The two of us were amazed that her father was in
intensive care for a month and a half, but didn't
pass away until after he had received the blessed
Green Scapular. We both felt sure that our
Blessed Mother obtained for him the grace of a
holy death.

~~~~~~~

My husband has a cousin Doris who lived
on Long Island, New York. Her daughter Kathy
called us from Florida one day, and told us her
mother was in the hospital, and not doing well at
all. In fact she thought she was dying. We knew
Doris had battled with breast cancer years
before, and we had given her one of our precious
scapulars when we had first found out about it.
We told her daughter we would go to see Doris,
and we decided to drive out to Long Island the
very next day.

When we arrived in the hospital at the
floor that Doris was on, behold, there was a
Catholic priest in a brown habit in the hallway.
We asked him to please visit Doris, hear her
confession, and get her ready to meet Our Lord.
We then went in to visit our cousin. In a little

while the priest came by and we left the room so they could talk. When the priest came out he said to us, "She's all set."

When we went back in, we asked Doris, who had just received Our Lord in Holy Communion, if she would like a blessed Brown Scapular. It was then that Doris showed us the Green Scapular around her neck that we had given her years before and told us she wouldn't be without it. She decided to put the brown one on also.

The next day Doris died, well taken care of by our Blessed Mother. How happy we were that we did not put off visiting Doris in the hospital that day, the day before she passed away. When we spoke to her daughters, Kathy & Laura, about our visit with their mother, they were very much consoled by all we told them.

~~~~~~~~

We have dear friends, Madelline and Ed, having known them for many years. It was through my Aunt Alma, who was visiting from Maine, that we came to meet them. None of us could get over the fact that Alma's friends lived down the street from us and we had never met them until she came to visit Madelline one afternoon. Alma kept telling her sister Julie the directions to Madelline's house, piece by piece. Finally, Julie asked what street she lived on. When Alma said the name of the street, Julie couldn't get over it! "That's the street Jackie and Eddie live on!" Julie could have driven there practically blindfolded! She and my Uncle Frank had been to our home a number of times.

I was in the backyard when my son Jack, who was about eight years old at the time, came running to get me. "Aunt Alma, Aunt Alma," he yelled. He was so excited! Now, I knew Alma was in town, but I never thought she'd have the time to come to visit us because she had her father, her sisters and brother to visit. I didn't know that she had also arranged to visit a friend she had worked with a long time ago. How happy I was to see Julie and Alma!

"I didn't come to see you," Alma said with a laugh, "I came to see my friend down the street." I asked her if her friend had a son named Randy. "Yes," she told me. I couldn't get over it, because our Jack had played once in a while with a boy named Randy who lived seven houses away, and I hadn't met his parents yet. And so, we all went down to visit Madelline. Eventually,

Madelline and I, our husbands and children, became very close friends.

Many years later Madelline and Ed moved to Virginia to be near their daughter Nancie, her husband and children who were now living down there. We used to visit them on our way to our timeshare in Florida. When Ed was about eighty years old he suffered a stroke but recuperated very nicely. The next time we went to see them I offered Ed a blessed Green Scapular, and told him about our son-in-law Billy's experience with leukemia and how he wore the scapular for a couple of months. Ed, even though he wasn't Catholic, he was of a Protestant denomination, graciously accepted the scapular and put it in his pocket. The next time I spoke to Madelline on the telephone she started to tell me, "You know, Jackie, ever since you gave Ed that scapular, he's been wearing it. I never question him about it," she said.

A couple of years later during one of our phone conversations, she told me the scapular broke and Ed tied it back together and put it on again. Well, the next time we visited, Ed walked us to the car when we were ready to leave. I mentioned to him that Madelline told me the scapular had broken and that he made a knot so he could keep wearing it. I offered him a few more. He seemed delighted and said, "These will last me till I die." Then he told me, "I feel better with it on, and I kiss it every morning."

A few years later Ed passed away from other complications. Madelline told me that Ed wore the scapular till the day he died. Of course my husband and I went to Virginia to be with our friend and her family for the wake and funeral. After the service there were about seven cars that went to the cemetery. That particular cemetery did not allow fresh flowers on the graves. They were only permitted at the burial site when there was a new internment. Other graves were adorned with artificial flowers.

After the prayers were said at the grave site, my husband and I started walking to our car. It was a very windy day. Next to our car door was an artificial red rose that had blown over from one of the other graves. Ours was the only car that had a flower blown over to it! I felt it was from Ed, thanking us for the gift of the Green Scapular and I felt sure that our Blessed Mother helped him to prepare to meet her son Jesus. I gratefully picked up the rose, brought it home, and treasured it as something special from Ed.

The wife of one of the couples we met through the Marriage Encounter experience told me her mother was seriously ill and in the hospital. She was happy to accept a Green Scapular to bring to her mother. The next time I saw her, she told me, "Jackie, when I brought the Green Scapular to my mother I felt the Blessed Mother's presence in the room!" How happy we both were that Our Lady made her presence known. We both felt sure that her mother received very special blessings that day.

My husband and I used to own a summer place in the Catskill Mountains in New York State, and while we were staying there one summer, my husband was in need of a new hearing aid. We found a hearing aid specialist we both liked very much, and during one of our conversations he mentioned that his wife had a serious health problem. I asked him if she would accept a Green Scapular. He readily took it, telling me his wife was Catholic; he was Jewish. Every time we saw him after that we would ask how his wife was doing. He always told us she was doing well. Eventually we sold that summer home to buy one closer to our children so it would be easier for them to visit.

About five years after we moved to our new summer home, we decided to return to our old spot in the Catskills. We visited a couple of our previous neighbors and before we left the area my husband wanted to see his former hearing aid specialist in town. I stayed in the car while my husband went in to see if he could find him in the new office building where he was now located. To my surprise when my husband Ed came out he asked me, "Jackie, do you have a Green Scapular on you?" Our Jewish friend wanted one for his car! He said he lost the one I had given him and he was so happy to see Ed in the hopes he could get another one. I had forgotten that I offered a scapular to him when I gave him one for his sick wife. How happy we were that we had stopped by!

~~~~~~~

For many years Ed took care of our lawn; the mowing, raking of leaves, etc., until he hurt his back when doing this yardwork, and he was out of work for two weeks. It was then that he realized he had to hire a gardener.

Let's say the gardener's name was Tony. He and his men took a load off Eddie's back (no pun intended), and did a great job of taking care of our lawn. One day I offered Tony a Green Scapular and he graciously took it. It was either then or at another time that he told me he and his wife had nine children. She had been married before and was hoping that Tony, to whom she was civilly married, would be willing to have her apply for an annulment of her first marriage and then get married in the Church. She went to Mass every Sunday but didn't receive Holy Communion, he told me, because she was divorced and remarried outside the Church. He was a lapsed Catholic, and had no interest in her applying for an annulment. Quite a bit of time passed when Tony shared with me that he gave into his wife, she got an annulment, and they were married in the Church. I had never seen such a look of peaceful happiness on his face, as Tony shared all of this with me. How happy I was to hear this good news! Praise be to the Blessed Mother who helps to change hearts!

~~~~~~~

Whenever one of our grandchildren decides to buy a car, we give him or her a Green Scapular to put in the car to ask our Blessed Mother's protection. I tell them it's not a good luck charm, and ask them to say a little prayer to Our Lady when they drive. Of course we also have one in our car, and how many times I've wondered, "How didn't that car hit us?" Thank you Mother for all the times you have watched over our family!

Between the adults and the grandchildren, three cars have overturned, one of which was totaled; three other cars were totaled; one car skidded into the oncoming lane, and another slid right across a well-traveled road. Thank God no car was coming in either direction, and no one in any of the cars was seriously injured. Praise God!

~~~~~~~~

Our dear friends, Dottie and Norrie who are Episcopalian, also treasure the Green Scapulars we have given them. Dottie keeps one in her handbag and Norrie carries one in his pocket. They also have one in their car. They are very grateful for the protection given them by our Blessed Mother.

While traveling on the highway to Florida one day, they suddenly approached a steel girder lying in the road which they could not avoid. They hit the girder, the tire was destroyed, but fortunately no other damage was done to the car. They were amazed and very thankful. Fortunately they were near an exit, and a Good Samaritan stopped and took Norrie to a phone, (this was before cell phones!), so he could call for assistance. The tire was replaced and they were able to continue on their way.

Upon traveling home from their daughter's home in Maine after a Christmas visit, they skidded on black ice and slammed into a telephone pole, which in retrospect they were grateful for, because it stopped them from going any further. If they hadn't hit the pole they would have gone down a ravine. Their car was totaled but they were glad to be alive.

Norrie did suffer two broken ribs but did not need to be hospitalized and was able to recuperate at their daughter's home. As Dottie said, "We could have been killed." They were very grateful to Our Lord and His Blessed Mother.

The devil hates the Green Scapular. Through our Blessed Mother's powerful intercession and prayerful confidence in her, she has freed many a soul from his grip. When we had our summer place in the Catskills years ago, a woman in the area told me the following story.

As a mother she was very concerned about the type of friends her son was hanging around with. One day one of her son's friends whom she was concerned about came to visit. They proceeded to go to her son's room to talk, and shortly thereafter her son's friend left the house. She asked her son, "How come your friend left so quickly?" "Mom," he said, "the strangest thing happened." We sat on the bed to talk, and my friend suddenly jumped up and said, "I hate that bed, I hate that bed," and then proceeded to sit in the chair on the other side of the room. Soon after, he left.

"Son," she answered, "come with me." She led the way back to her son's bedroom and lifted up his mattress to show him what she had previously placed there, a blessed Green Scapular.

It makes one think that this so-called "friend" was more than likely into the occult for him to react so strongly to the presence of a blessed Green Scapular hidden under a mattress.

Anyone wanting to purchase a Green Scapular may contact:

The National Shrine of Saint Elizabeth Ann Seton, 339 S. Seton Avenue, Emmitsburg, MD 21727. 301-447-6606 or www.setonshrine.org

HE HEARD A VOICE

When the Our Lady of Medjugorje prayer group first began at the parish house of St. Thomas Aquinas Church in Forestburgh, New York, Ed and I were among those present. It was decided that we would meet weekly in the evening. Our pastor, Father Robert J. McCabe was with us at almost every meeting and made himself available for anyone who wanted to go to confession. Ed went to the parish of St. Mary's in Port Jervis, N.Y. with a flyer containing the information about the newly formed prayer group. He met some people outside of Mass and invited them to join us. A few of them accepted the invitation, became regular members and were a great addition to the group.

How well I remember when one of the members, Joe, told some of us that he had been away from the church for a long time. He had recently moved from New York City to Cuddebackville, N.Y., outside of Port Jervis. One morning, he related, he was lying in bed and heard a voice say, "Go to church." He didn't even know where the church was, he confessed. But after hearing that voice he made it his business to find out.

Joe came back to Mass and the sacraments and began going to Mass daily. He became an extraordinary minister of Holy Communion and an altar server whenever they needed one.

Joe became very active in the Right to Life movement. He was president of Orange County Right to Life for two terms. He attended the March for Life in Washington, D.C., held in January, a number of times. In October of 2008 Joe said that St. Mary's Parish would sponsor a bus to D.C. the following year. How right he was! Even though he passed away in November, the following January, 2009, the parish organized a bus trip and has done so every year since.

Joe picketed and prayed at Planned Parenthood in Newburgh, Goshen and Monroe. He also became a member of the Knights of Columbus.

Joe worked for Pan American Airlines in Queens, N.Y. He got up at five o'clock in the morning to start the long drive to the airport. On the way home he stopped at St. Mary's Church to join in praying the nightly Rosary at 7 p.m. It was only after the Rosary that he went home for dinner.

How faithful and full of good works was Joe after that glorious morning when "he heard a voice."

"Oh, that today you would hear his voice:
'Harden not your hearts…….'"
(Psalm 95:7-8)

LIFE IN THE SPIRIT

Many years ago I attended a Life in the Spirit Seminar at Sacred Heart Church in Yonkers, N.Y. At the conclusion of the seminar the priest prayed over each of the participants to receive the Baptism of the Holy Spirit. This invocation of the Holy Spirit is in addition to the sacraments of Baptism and Confirmation. It is a renewal of the graces received in these sacraments. A number of the people who go to these seminars become involved in the Catholic Charismatic Renewal which as of the year 2017 is celebrating its Golden Anniversary. I've attended a Charismatic prayer group in the past led by a deacon in one of our Catholic churches and found it very uplifting. I've also attended Catholic Charismatic Retreats and found them most helpful.

Pope Paul V1 encouraged those who attended the International Conference on the Catholic Charismatic renewal in 1975 in their renewal efforts, especially to remain anchored in the Church. Pope John Paul II, speaking to international leaders in 1979 said he was convinced that this movement is a very important component of the entire renewal of the Church.

Cardinal Joseph Ratzinger who later became Pope acknowledged the good occurring in the Charismatic Renewal and provided some cautions. Pope Francis has also endorsed the Charismatic Renewal.

Becoming involved in the life of the Church in any of its many areas should always lead us into a deeper relationship with Our Lord in the Holy Sacrifice of the Mass, the Sacrament of Reconciliation, our Blessed Mother and the teachings of the Church.

SAINT JOSEPH, THE FOSTER FATHER OF JESUS

When we bought a summer home in the Catskills near Monticello, N.Y. we enjoyed having the children and grandchildren visit, but because it was almost two hours away it made the trip more desirable for them if they could stay over for a night or two. As the grandchildren got older and involved in sports on the weekends it was difficult for them to come and visit, so we decided to sell the house and get a place closer to the family. The year was 2001. We had difficulty selling the house even though we had prayed.

On March 19, 2002, on the feast of St. Joseph, I decided to make a novena every hour to St. Joseph. The next day the house was sold. Praise to St. Joseph! The person who bought our home had seen it before, but after the events of 9/11 he wasn't sure if his job was stable. When he called our real estate broker on March 20, 2002, he told her he wanted to buy our house! She asked him if he would like to see it again, and he said no. He remembered it well, and now that his job was stable he would like to go ahead with the purchase. We thought it was pretty amazing, that he didn't even want to look at it for a second time before he decided to definitely buy the house.

St. Joseph has answered many of our prayers. St. Teresa of Avila was a great advocate of his. St. Joseph, because he was the foster father of Jesus, she knew by experience, that when he presents our petitions to Our Lord his intercession is very powerful. She asked others to recommend themselves to St. Joseph, and they too, knew the same thing by experience. So many have received favors from him.

Prayer to St. Joseph

This prayer is said to been founded in the fiftieth year of Our Lord and Savior Jesus Christ.

"O St. Joseph, whose protection is so great, so strong, so prompt before the throne of God, I place in you all my interests and desires. O St. Joseph, do assist me by your powerful intercession and obtain for me from your divine Son all spiritual blessings through Jesus Christ our Lord; so that having engaged here below your heavenly power, I may offer my thanksgiving and homage to the most loving of Fathers. O St. Joseph, I never weary contemplating you and Jesus asleep in your arms. I dare not approach while He reposes near your heart. Press Him in my name and kiss His fine head for me, and ask Him to return the kiss when I draw my dying breath. St. Joseph, patron of departing souls, pray for me. Amen."

(Imprimatur: Most Rev. George W. Ahr, Bishop of Trenton)

Memorare to St. Joseph

"Remember, O most pure spouse of the Virgin Mary, St. Joseph, my beloved patron, that never has it been heard that anyone sought your aid without being comforted. Inspired by this confidence, I come to you and fervently commend myself to you. Despise not my petition, dear foster father of our Redeemer, but graciously accept it. Amen."

St. Joseph has two feast days: March 19, "St. Joseph, the husband of Mary," and May 1, "St. Joseph, the Worker."

MY FATHER'S DEATH

When I was only a year and a half old, my father, John Dykes Mee, Jr. passed away of complications after surgery. Believe it or not I have one memory of him. He was operated on in February of 1935. He came home from the hospital on one of those unusually warm days that we sometimes get in January or February. My sister Dorothy and I were playing together in a vestibule off the kitchen the day my father came home. My mother called us out to the backyard where he was resting in a lounge chair. We ran out to see him and I remember hugging him and him hugging me back.

Many years later, after my sister and I were married, Ed and I were visiting at her home. I asked her if what I remembered was a true memory and she confirmed that it was. At first my sister didn't want me to go on, (I'm sure she thought that having a memory at so young an age was impossible). But my brother-in-law Charlie interjected, "let her speak" and I was very grateful. Dot, as I now call her, is four years older than I and recalled that day very well. I even remember my mother standing off to the left where my father was resting in the lounge chair.

Before my mother and father were married he became a Catholic. After a while, he fell away from practicing his faith. When he was home about a week after his operation, he experienced acute pain and was rushed back to the hospital. They opened him up and found he was full of gangrene. All they could do was close the incision and wait for the inevitable. My mother was beside herself with grief! They were both in their twenties. It was my Protestant grandmother, God bless her, knowing her son was now Catholic, who asked the nurse to get a priest for my father.

My mother told me in later years that it was my father's friend, a doctor, who drove him to the hospital to see what had gone wrong. One day, about twenty five years later during an office visit to the same doctor, (he was still in practice), I asked him to tell me if my father had any idea that he might die. The doctor remembered the day vividly. He told me my father had said, "Charlie, don't let me die." So it was evident to me that he thought that death was a possibility. His pain must have been that great. He told me also that they kept my father under sedation until he passed away.

Years later, I received in the mail from the Carmelites, a Perpetual Mass Enrollment in the Society of the Little Flower of Jesus, Saint Thérèse. I decided to enroll my father, and a few others to benefit in the prayers, Masses and sacrifices of the Carmelite Order, past, present and future. I placed my father's name first on the list. I sent the names for the enrollment with a donation to the Carmelite Order. A couple of weeks later I received a response from one of the Carmelite priests that he had received my request to enroll those I mentioned and I received a lovely card with a picture of St. Thérèse and the roses. It was signed March 3rd, the day of my father's death! How pleased I was to see that was the day he was enrolled. I hadn't any thought in my mind that the anniversary of my father's death was coming up when I enrolled him in the Society of St. Thérèse!

ST. THÉRÈSE AND THE ROSES

Marie-Francois Thérèse was born in Alencon, France on January 2, 1873. She was baptized two days later in the Church of Notre Dame; her eldest sister, Marie, was her godmother.

St. Thérèse was the youngest of nine children of exemplary parents, Zelie and Louis Martin, who were canonized as saints by Pope Francis in Rome, on October 18, 2015. Four of the children died at an early age, but of the rest, one entered the Visitation Convent at Caen, Thérèse and her other three sisters became cloistered, Carmelite Sisters at Lisieux, France.

Four years after Thérèse's birth, her mother died and the family moved to Lisieux. At fifteen, she entered Carmel with special permission from the Bishop and was named Sister Thérèse of the Child Jesus and of the Holy Face. At the solemn examination before her Profession as a Sister, she declared her reason for coming to Carmel, "I have come to save souls and above all to pray for priests."

Her autobiography was written under obedience, and it was only after her death that it was decided to let it go beyond the walls of the convent. The nine years she spent in the convent seemed very ordinary, but her writings proved they were quite extraordinary. She was told to write down all of her childhood memories. These were included with the rest of her life in the convent. All were published after her death, as a book, "The Story of a Soul." It had tremendous impact on the Christian world. Sister Thérèse's "little way" of spiritual childhood of the acceptance of God's holy will, of trust in His merciful love, in the offering of little sacrifices, acts of kindness, her daily duties, and her sufferings, with love, for the salvation of souls, has inspired many people to imitate her "little way."

She wrote, "To pick up a pin for love can convert a soul." She preferred, "The monotony of obscure sacrifice to all ecstasies." She remained at Carmel until her death at the age of twenty-four. During the last year of her life she slowly wasted away from tuberculosis. Yet shortly before she died, on September 30, she whispered, "I would not suffer less." She stated: "I want to spend my heaven doing good on earth."

Favors and graces without number have

been attributed to her intercession. She herself said, before she died, she would let fall a "shower of roses from Heaven." She was canonized a saint on May 17, 1925. She is the patroness of the missions and was declared a Doctor of the Church in 1997 by Pope John Paul II. There are 33 Doctors of the Church. The title is given to certain saints whose writings and teachings are helpful to Christians "in any age of the Church." Her feast day is October 1st.

The day after I began to write about St. Thérèse, one of our parishioners, Mary Frank, came into the Chapel and sat near my husband and me. She then proceeded to place a red rose in my bag. After Mass she told me she had meant to bring the rose to our Cenacle prayer group a few nights before, but forgot. As she was leaving her home to come to Mass, she noticed the rose laying on her dining room table. She said she felt moved to bring it to church and give it to me. She apologized that the rose wasn't as fresh and beautiful as it was when she meant to bring it, a few days before, but how beautiful it was to me! I felt like it was a gift from St. Thérèse, for spreading her little way of spiritual childhood.

Ever since I was a young child I had a devotion to her. My grandparents had a number of religious books in one of their cabinets in their dining room. Among them was the life of St. Thérèse with beautiful pictures of her as a child, with long blonde hair, alongside her father; one of her First Holy Communion Day, and pictures of her as a Carmelite nun. I loved looking at the pictures when I was little and so I naturally took her name for my Confirmation name, when I was confirmed in the second grade. Years later I read "The Story of a Soul" and found it interesting, delightful and very easy to read.

The first time I ever heard of anyone receiving roses after praying to St. Thérèse, was from our friend Sister Winnie, whom we met through the Marriage Encounter Community. Many a Marriage Encounter weekend were held at the Immaculate Conception Motherhouse of the Sisters of St. Francis in Hastings on Hudson, New York. It was there that we met Sister Winifred Denise, O.S.F. whom almost everyone affectionately called "Sister Winnie." Winnie was in charge of making the couples who came to make a weekend, welcome and at ease. She was there to serve them in any way she could. Everyone loved her. She prayed for them all, but she always picked out a special couple to pray a little extra for, and she would tell them that they were her "special couple" for that weekend. They were always very grateful.

Eventually Sister Winnie, Ed and I became very good friends. One summer afternoon we had Winnie over for a cookout. After dinner we were sitting outside in our portable screened in porch. It was a beautiful evening and Winnie started to tell us about her strong devotion to St. Thérèse, the Little Flower of Jesus. "I took Theresa for my Confirmation name," I told her, "and I love her too!" She started to tell Ed and me about the times she received roses in answer to prayers she offered to St. Thérèse. Winnie told us of the time she suffered from a severe stomach ulcer. She had to have an operation, and the doctor removed three quarters of her stomach. Winnie went down to seventy seven pounds! She prayed to St. Thérèse that if Our Lord wanted to take her that was fine with her, but if she was going to live would Thérèse please send her a rose as a sign that she would survive.

Soon after, another Sister came into her room with a vase full of flowers. She told Sister Winnie that one of the visitors at the hospital had given her the flowers and asked that they be given to a child. The sister told Winnie, "Sister you are young at heart, and I thought I would bring the flowers to you." Winnie thanked her and then she noticed, in the middle of the flowers were three beautiful roses! She felt that Thérèse had answered her prayer. Sure enough, Winnie recovered!

As we listened to a couple of other stories from Winnie I said, "Humph, St. Thérèse never sent *me* any roses!"

~~~~~~~~~

One day I was at the 12 o'clock Mass at Immaculate Conception Church in Tuckahoe, New York. Looking back, I know I was given a very special grace that day. I was praying with all my heart to Our Lord for everyone I ever knew. Distractions didn't seem to be a problem for me as I was praying that day, whereas, so often, I have to bring my thoughts back to the prayers that are being said by the priest and the people present. About 1:30 P.M. our time, our dear friends Madelline and Ed's son Randy was killed in an automobile accident in Phoenix, Arizona. Ed and I didn't find out about it until about eight or nine o'clock that night. We were at another couple's house at a Marriage

Encounter meeting, when our son Jack and our daughter Diane came to the house to tell us the awful news. We left the meeting immediately to be with Madelline and Ed, as the couples promised to pray. How extremely sad we were and how difficult it was to see them in such grief. There was not much we could do except to be present to them during this so sorrowful a time. Ed and I felt so sad for our friends in their great loss. We shared their grief also, having known Randy since he was in grammar school!

The next morning I was lying in bed and in my heart desired a rose that I could bring to Madelline and Ed as a sign that Randy was either in heaven or on the way (we call it Purgatory). Later that morning our five year old daughter Elizabeth came to me. "Mommy, look what Karen has for you!" Karen was a little girl about four years old who lived close by in the neighborhood. She had never brought me anything before that day. She handed me some flowers and I said, "Thank you so much Karen, they're beautiful!" They were pretty little pink flowers. As I held them in my hand I felt a furry feeling on the stems. I thought, "Could these be roses?" I looked at the stems, and sure enough there were the thorns! Karen had given me a beautiful cluster of lovely pink roses! I cried a lot of tears, and was full of gratitude as I realized that St. Thérèse had answered my unspoken prayer. I had only desired the roses in my heart! I quickly called the florist and changed our order of flowers for Randy's funeral to a basket of pink roses instead of what I originally had ordered. I knew I had to tell my friend Madelline all of this, but I wondered how she would accept it, because she is not of our Catholic faith! That evening my husband and I went to see Madelline and Ed, and I told them everything that happened. They listened quietly, and then Madelline said as she took the roses from me, "I wish they would last forever!"

The next day a friend who was a member of her church came to visit her. When Madelline told her about the roses, her friend told her she would dry them for her as this was one of her hobbies. She dried the roses and put them in a glass dome with a wooden bottom. She did a beautiful job and they looked lovely. Madelline got her wish! She was much comforted by these roses brought by a little four year old girl to her friend's mother who had desired them in her heart. On the day of Randy's funeral, before we left the cemetery, Madelline chose to bring home from the grave site a couple of pink roses from the basket of roses that we had sent to the funeral parlor for Randy's wake. Upon seeing this, I was much comforted that they meant so much to her.

When I told my cleaning woman, who was from San Salvador, of all that had happened, she said that in her country they call the small roses like the ones I received, "Thérèses!"

A few months later I phoned Madelline, as I often did. She told me the strangest thing happened that day as she was passing Randy's cemetery on her way to work. All of a sudden she smelled the aroma of roses in her car! There were no flowers around and she didn't understand where the scent was coming from. I said, "Madelline, do you know what today is?" "No," she answered. I had been to Mass that morning, and that day, I told her, was the feast day of St. Thérèse! How wonderful to get another sign from heaven that Randy was being well taken care of! What a gift it was from the Holy Spirit to inspire me to pray so diligently at Mass for everyone I ever knew, on the day Randy died, in that tragic car accident.

St. Thérèse has also blessed our family by her intercession. Our daughter Mary Thérèse and her husband Gene had one daughter, Marianne. Our first grandchild was a girl, Jennifer. How happy we were to be grandparents! Then we had eight grandsons in a row! Of course each one was very special to us and the family, but when Marianne was born, even the grandsons were thrilled!

Mary and Gene had been hoping for quite some time for another baby but were unable to conceive. So Mary began a novena, (nine days of prayer) to St. Thérèse, her patron saint, to ask her intercession with Our Lord that they might have another child. As she was praying the novena on the fourth day, little four-year-old Marianne came into the room saying, "Look, Mommy, I have a flower for you." When Mary looked down at her daughter, she saw that she was carrying a small bouquet of pink artificial roses which had been in Marianne's bedroom. Immediately, Mary knew that St. Thérèse was answering her prayers and was sending her a rose through Marianne. She asked her daughter, "Why did you bring me that flower?" knowing that it had been in her room for years. "I don't know," Marianne replied. Without her realizing it, she was inspired to be God's instrument for a message of hope and love to her parents.

When Mary told me what had happened, I asked her if she had mentioned to Marianne that she was making a novena to St. Thérèse. Mary answered, "No." I then asked her if Marianne knew that St. Thérèse sometimes sends a rose in answer to prayer. Again Mary answered, "No." Before long we heard the wonderful news that Mary and Gene were expecting their second child, whom they named Rose Kathleen. Because Mary's middle name was Thérèse, she did not want it to sound like she was naming both her children after herself, so she had promised St. Thérèse to name the baby Rose, her little Rose from St. Thérèse, if the baby was a girl. We were all very grateful that St. Thérèse interceded before God for this most special Rose, who is a wonderful addition to the family.

Prayer to St. Thérèse

O little Thérèse of the child Jesus, please pick for me a rose from the heavenly gardens and send it to me as a message of love. O little flower of Jesus, ask God today to grant the favors I now place with confidence in your hands. (Mention your request). St. Thérèse, help me always to believe as you did, in God's great love for me, so that I might imitate your "little way" each day. Amen.

The Martin family home in Lisieux, France

*Statuary in the rear garden of the Martin home
of Thérèse asking her father for his permission
to enter Carmel at age fifteen*

A PILGRIMAGE TO LOURDES AND ROME

In 1975 Pope Paul VI proclaimed a Holy Year. The Marriage Encounter people organized a ten day pilgrimage to Lourdes and Rome and even then the price was cheap, only $530.00!! And that included airfare, land travel, hotel, breakfast and dinner, etc. How excited I was when Ed said we could go!

Once a month we had an M.E. Renewal night in our parish. Our friend Sister Winnie, welcomed and cared for the couples making the Marriage Encounter weekends in the Motherhouse of her Order, the Sisters of St. Francis. We knew she would just love to go to Lourdes and Rome with us and the other couples, priests and religious who were going. We decided to raise funds to pay for her trip. We asked the couples who came to the renewal nights if they would like to contribute to a fund to help Sister Winnie join us. "No amount is too small," we told them. I mentioned that if they weren't able to make a contribution that particular night, but wanted to help, if they gave us their name and address I would eventually send them a reminder letter.

A couple of weeks before we left for the pilgrimage, we counted up the money we had collected for Winnie and it was less than $250.00. Sister Winnie was really concerned. She was afraid, and rightly so, that Ed and I would want to chip in the rest of the amount, which would have been okay with us, but we wouldn't have minded some extra help either. Well anyway, I decided to send our reminder letter, saying once more that no amount was too small to send if they still wanted to help. A few days before the pilgrimage, I counted up all the money that had come in. We collected $531.00!! One dollar more than the cost of the trip, and we hadn't contributed anything to the fund yet! How good God is! He really put his stamp of approval on Sister Winnie joining us by inspiring the couples to give just the amount that was needed, plus one dollar!

Altogether from the United States there were approximately 2,500 Marriage Encounter people going. Our group also included priests, sisters, and we knew at least one or two brother religious, there may have been more, who joined us. And what a wonderful trip it was! Ed and I experienced, as did those around us, so many graces and blessings from Our Lord and His

Blessed Mother on that pilgrimage.

When we were in Lourdes, Sister Winnie bought us a lovely wooden rosary which we had blessed by the Pope when we were in Rome. She also purchased a large candle and asked the caretaker at the outdoor chapel at Lourdes to place it at the top of a tree of candles in the grotto, the cave where Our Lady appeared to St. Bernadette. Sister Winnie then wrote a note and attached it to the bottom of the candle asking our Blessed Mother to bless Ed and me, and all the couples who helped her to go on the pilgrimage.

What an experience it was to go into the baths at Lourdes! I felt so blessed and renewed. I cried, and felt so much love for everyone around me! The candlelight procession in the evening, in honor of Our Lady, was very moving. Imagine 2,500 people singing hymns, each one holding a lit candle, processing reverently with a statue of our Blessed Mother that was being carried on a platform covered with flowers. The hymns were sung with so much love!

Most of the miracles that have been reported at Lourdes have occurred during the blessing of the sick, when the priest blesses the people with the monstrance containing Our Lord Jesus in the Most Blessed Sacrament. In fact, when we arrived home from our trip, we found out that while our group was in Rome there was a great miracle in Lourdes that was reported in the French newspapers. One of our friends who came with us on pilgrimage had a cousin in France who told her of the news article. A woman who had been paralyzed since birth rose from her stretcher during the blessing of the sick and walked!

~~~~~~~~~~

It was on February 11, 1858, that Bernadette Soubirous, while hunting for firewood with her sister and a friend, hesitated because of her asthma, to cross a stream that the girls had already crossed. All of a sudden, in a grotto nearby, she saw a Lady wearing a white dress with a blue sash and a yellow rose resting on each foot. Immediately Bernadette reached for the rosary in her pocket, but couldn't begin to raise her arm to bless herself until the Lady in the vision, without moving her lips, moved her fingers along the rosary she was holding. When Bernadette finished her rosary the vision disappeared. This was the first of eighteen apparitions.

Our Lady told Bernadette on February 18

when she appeared to her at the grotto, "I do not promise to make you happy in this world, but in the next." On February 24 the message given was one of penance. Our Lady repeated the word "Penitence!" three times to her and told her, "Pray for the conversion of sinners." She also asked her if she would, "kiss the ground in penance for the conversion of sinners," which Bernadette willingly did. On February 25, Our Lady told her to "Go and drink at the spring and wash in it......."

On the feast day of the Annunciation, March 25, when Bernadette having been asked by the parish priest, to ask the Lady's name, Our Lady responded, "I am the Immaculate Conception." In order to remember the title Our Lady gave her, Bernadette had to keep repeating this to herself as she ran to tell the priest Our Lady's response. The eighteenth apparition took place on July 16, the feast of Our Lady of Mount Carmel.

Crowds of people had already been coming to the grotto and miracles had taken place from the spring of water that appeared after Our Lady told Bernadette to dig into the earth during the ninth apparition on February 25.

Bernadette entered the convent of the

Sisters of Charity of Nevers, France in 1866 and died in 1879 at the age of 35 after suffering a number of illnesses including tuberculosis of the leg. Bernadette wrote, "I want my whole life to be inspired by love." She was canonized a saint by Pope Pius XI on December 8, 1933. Her body lies incorrupt in a glass casket where she looks peacefully asleep in the convent at Nevers.

~~~~~~~~~~

We stayed three days in Lourdes and then boarded a train to Rome. How awed we felt when we approached Vatican City and saw the Dome of St. Peter's in the distance! How magnificent and expansive it was! We never comprehended from the pictures we had seen just how majestic it looked!

We visited the four major basilicas: St. John Lateran, St. Mary Major, St. Paul Outside the Walls, and of course, St. Peter's. Each one had its own importance and unique treasures from the past. When we entered St. Peter's we were struck with reverence. What a gift it was to behold Michelangelo's Pieta carved out of magnificent white Carrara marble!

During the Holy Year there were

countless numbers of people in Rome. What an event it was when 2,500 people plus those Marriage Encounter couples from Europe who had joined us, went through the Holy Door at St. Peter's Basilica, singing exultantly! The "Holy Door" is opened only when a Holy Year is proclaimed by the Pope, usually every 25 years. The people of Rome, because of our enthusiastic singing, began to call us "the alleluia people!" Some of them joined us at Mass and we were happy to welcome them.

We had an outdoor audience in St. Peter's Square with Pope Paul VI. When the Marriage Encounter Group was announced to him, what an uproar there was in salutation of our beloved Pope! He responded by vigorously waving his two hands in greeting to us.

It was when we were leaving the square that we met a priest who later became a dear friend, Rev. Gérard J. Breault, O.M.V. At first I was not much interested in speaking to him because we were looking for our friends whom we were supposed to meet after the pope's audience. All of a sudden though, we spotted our friends disappearing in the distance and I felt "stuck" with this priest to whom I didn't want to be impolite by running after our friends. Little did I know at the time, that meeting Fr. Breault was one of our good Lord's best gifts to us. And so I decided to make good use of meeting this priest and asked him if he knew where Cardinal Wright's office was. We had the key to the City of Yonkers, given to us by a friend involved in politics, to give to the pope. We had heard that we should bring the key to Cardinal Wright's office and the cardinal would give the key to the pope. Fr. Breault tried to explain to us where the office was, but then he decided to bring us there himself. This priest was so filled with joy! We arranged to meet him again on one of our free days and discovered that he was born and raised in Canada and sometimes visited friends in the New York area. We asked him to come to visit us if he should come to the States, which he eventually did. Being with this joyous priest made me think of what St. John Bosco, the founder of the Salesians, must have been like to those who met him. When I had read about him years before, either from the book "Give Me Souls" or from a pamphlet of the same title about his life, the joy of his spirit and his strong desire to save souls touched me. Three of our children went to camps for a couple of weeks in the summer run by the Salesians and loved it. Our son Jack, to the camp for boys in West Haverstraw, N.Y. and our daughters, Mary and Elizabeth to Camp Auxilium in Newton, N.J.

When we got home from our trip Ed asked me, "Let's start the day by saying the Rosary together every morning." Wow! For him to ask me that question was, as far as I was concerned, a little miracle from Our Lady of Lourdes! Sometimes our young daughter Elizabeth came into our bedroom to join us in this very powerful prayer.

~~~~~~~~~

When we came back from our pilgrimage something very special happened. A former neighbor of ours, a wonderful Jewish woman, had been suffering from the disease Lupus and its side effects for a long time. She had been enduring much pain from passing large blood clots from her urinary tract. We prayed for her at Lourdes. I brought home a large bottle of water from the miraculous spring there. We got home from our pilgrimage late at night. I looked out my window about two a.m. and saw that Rachel's bedroom light was on and I knew she must be in pain.

The next day I brought my entire bottle of

Lourdes water to my Jewish friend. I'd hoped she would accept our gift and use it for her benefit. Lo and behold, she told me sometime later that she drank it all at the advice of her Jewish mother-in-law! The blood clots stopped and she was much better for quite some time.

After a couple of years or so, Rachel became seriously ill. The doctors told her husband he would be widowed soon after the beginning of the New Year. Rachel had a sore in her thigh that went right down to her bone so that her bone was visible, the wound was so deep. She was very ill.

Fr. Breault had come for a visit. Our friend Rachel was in a hospital in New Jersey and our priest friend was planning to go to New Jersey with another priest for a special meeting. I was so concerned about Rachel that I got up the nerve to ask our friend if he would go to see her in the hospital. What a good priest! He said yes, even though he never met Rachel! Father always had with him a special relic of our Blessed Mother Mary. It was a small piece of her veil and was enclosed in a small reliquary. The larger piece of Our Lady's veil, I found out sometime later, is kept in the Cathedrale Notre-Dame de Chartres, fifty miles outside of Paris, France where, once a year, a procession is held, venerating the relic. It is said to have been given by Charlemagne who received it as a gift during a visit to Jerusalem.

Of course I asked my Jewish friend by phone, if it would be all right with her if Father visited her. She gave her permission and Father went to see her with the other priest. When they arrived at the hospital Rachel was not in her room. The nurse upon seeing the priests said to them, "You have the right room, but the wrong religion." They waited until Rachel was brought back to her room. She told me she liked Fr. Breault very much. His joy was noticed by everyone who met him. He visited with her and then blessed her with the relic. Very soon after, her sores healed up, her health got better, and when the New Year arrived she and her husband went on vacation to one of the Caribbean Islands. Her doctor called it a miracle! Thanks be to God and the intercession of our Blessed Mother Mary!!

I had lost touch with Rachel since she and her husband moved from the area a long time ago. In the fall of 2012, I was able to find her phone number and gave her a call. It was so good to talk to her and reminisce over the wonderful blessings she received over thirty-five years ago. Praise God!

~~~~~~~~~

On one of Fr. Breault's visits, he told us about his brother who was also a priest, Fr. Alphonse Breault, O.M.I. who had the gift of healing. Father told us of a woman whose one leg was shorter than the other. Fr. Alphonse placed the relic of Our Lady's veil, (which our friend received after his brother's death), on her shorter leg and prayed, and then the leg immediately grew longer to equal the length of the other leg! He told us that sometimes his brother traveled with a statue of Our Lady of Fatima that had been known to shed tears. I told Father that a number of years previously, we had read that there was going to be a special day in honor of our Blessed Mother at the Marian Shrine in West Haverstraw, New York. They were bringing in by helicopter, a statue of Our Lady of Fatima that had cried. My husband and I drove to the Shrine with four of our children to be present at the outdoor procession, rosary, and all the events that were planned.

The helicopter was late in coming, but when it finally arrived we went up close to greet

173

Our Lady's statue. I remember saying she looked so sad. There was a great crowd present that day to honor our Blessed Mother and we were guided by the ushers into a wide line to make room, so that the statute could be carried on a platform to be placed eventually, after the Rosary was said, near the main altar at the outdoor chapel where we would then have Mass.

The platform carrying the statute passed by from where we were standing and continued to go on ahead. All of a sudden the procession halted and then began to move backwards, with the statue of Our Lady stopping right in front of us. Then the priest led the people in praying the Rosary. What a gift this was for us! I remember also when the Rosary was prayed, the face on the statue looked happy and the sadness that I previously witnessed had changed.

When I told Fr. Breault what happened that day, his response was, "That was my brother!" (He had led the procession). And so, we once did see his brother, Fr. Alphonse, without ever realizing it, until Father told us that he was there at the Marian Shrine at the same time we were! What a blessing this day was for us and for everyone who made the effort to go to honor our Blessed Mother Mary.

Dome of St. Peter's Basilica in Rome

A PILGRIM'S JOURNEY TO HEALING AT LOURDES

One of our parishioners, Carol, graciously consented to writing down the events that took place during her pilgrimage to Lourdes, France for the glory of God and His Blessed Mother Mary. How happy and grateful I am to include her story in this book.

In the late 1970s, Carol was being treated by her doctor for psoriasis arthritis and it had been decided to treat her disease with gold injections which caused such a reaction that her platelets went so low she almost died. Carol spent the next year on huge dosages of prednisone pills to get her platelets back to normal. The doctor tried all kinds of medicine to stop the development of pain and joint attacks. Finally it was decided to give her three options. One was to take a cancer drug in hopes it would stop the terrible attacks on her body, the second was to live on high dosages of prednisone for as long as her body could tolerate it, and the final one was to accept the destruction of her joints and ligaments, use a wheelchair and be on pain medication. This was for her a very hard decision since the pain was so overbearing and

176

no one could touch any part of her body without causing her severe pain.

While Carol was thinking of her options, she picked up a Catholic newspaper and in it was an ad for a pilgrimage to Lourdes, France. It was being led by Fr. Charest, a Montfort Father from Bayshore, Long Island, in New York. Accompanying the tour would be doctors and nurses to help the sick. Fr. Charest brought the sick on pilgrimage to Lourdes every year. Carol's decision was to accept the wheelchair and pain pills as this would allow her to care for her boys. She called the number provided, explained her condition, and said she would like to go with them. She felt she needed to go to visit her Mother Mary to ask her help to endure her pain and the way of life that she would now live. She truly believed that if she went to Lourdes Our Lady would help her. Fr. Charest had her doctor send him a report of her condition and asked Carol if she wanted a wheelchair and she said yes. The pilgrimage included four days in Dublin, Ireland and then four nights in Lourdes.

October 7th was the departure date and there were fifty-five pilgrims waiting to board the plane. They prayed a beautiful rosary to our Blessed Mother in honor of the feast of the Holy

Rosary which is celebrated by the Church on that day. Carol was assigned a roommate, Margaret, who helped her greatly as she had such difficulty in walking. On one of their days in Dublin, there was a side tour to Knock by bus. They traveled four hours each way.

Carol said that their visit to Our Lady of Knock was delightful. She sat in front of the altar that portrayed the wonderful Vision seen on August 21, 1879 in heavy rain by fifteen men, women and children on the gable of the parish church at Knock. The fifteen prayed in the drenching rain for hours until the Apparition ended.

The Vision was of an altar upon which was a lamb. Behind the lamb was a large Cross surrounded by angels. Looking directly at the Vision, to the left of the altar was St. John wearing a bishop's robes with a low mitre and an open book from which he seemed to preach though no words were spoken. To the left of St. John was Our Lady with her eyes and hands raised in prayer and on her head a gold crown with a rose. To Our Lady's left was St. Joseph with his hands joined together and his head bowed in prayer.

The first recorded cure at Knock came ten

days after the Apparition when a totally deaf young girl was healed when she knelt in prayer and applied some cement from the gable on her ear. After that there were hundreds of other cures and Knock has become a pilgrimage site for many.

Carol's group arrived at Knock a few days after Pope John Paul II's visit. The seats and stage were still set up. As they worshipped at Mass she felt her place in her Church and the Sacraments. It was beautiful there, and very special, a place visited by our Mother Mary, together with St. Joseph and St. John, and on the altar, the Lamb of God. She said, "Holiness was felt all over."

Carol's arthritis was so painful upon arriving back at the hotel that friends from the group had to help her to her room and to assist her in getting ready to retire. The pain was worse than she had ever experienced. The next night they departed for Lourdes and she explained to Fr. Charest that she needed a wheelchair waiting for her since she couldn't walk, she was so stiff. And so, at their arrival at Tarbes Airport she was greeted by her chair.

Margaret and another pilgrim, Bill, helped her quite a bit while she did the little bit of walking that she could manage. Her ankles would not support her standing, so each of them would take an arm and walk with her. By the second day Carol spent all her time in the wheelchair, but to her surprise one of their group, who was more ill than she, was the one to push and pull her each day. Carol believed the first healing or cure was that of allowing her to witness the depth of her pride. She gave a Sister and Father a hard time getting into the chair as she didn't think it was right for this Sister to have to take care of her. She had hoped one of the hospital volunteers would do this. But finally, Fr. Charest insisted that she accept Sister's help, and in obedience to him, she did.

Most of the people who know her, Carol admitted, knew the kind of chatterbox she usually is, but on this particular day she was silent all day long. "God helped me see the great pride I had and the truth behind why I didn't want Sister's help." They talked about it that night at dinner. Fr. Charest enjoyed hearing all about her day. She thanked God for this most precious gift that He gave her and it helped her to become vulnerable in asking for help and letting others see inside herself. "It was awesome," Carol said. She shared even further, "I often recall that day and to me it was indeed the biggest cure of Lourdes, I truly was cleansed interiorly."

When others know of a trip like this, they often asked you to bring petitions of theirs with you, and of course Carol who would not refuse anyone, left with quite a lot of them. Some wanted them placed in the grotto where Our Lady appeared, some in the baths. A priest friend of hers had a letter in an envelope that he asked her to place in the bath waters and she told him she would.

The day she entered the bath with his envelope, she plunged it into the water. When she got up the envelope was perfectly dry, nor did the ink run on the paper. "It was something to see!" Not only was the envelope completely dry, but so was she! And the volunteers had plunged her all the way into the waters.

The Basilica of the Immaculate Conception in Lourdes is magnificent to see. On the ground level is the Rosary Basilica surmounted by its dome on which sits the crown of Our Lady. There are ramps on either side to get to the crypt and the main Basilica. Beneath the main Basilica, in the crypt, there was Adoration of the Blessed Sacrament. This was one of Carol's favorite places to go. There she would sit and visit with Jesus in the quiet and stillness of His Presence. It was quite damp and chilly there and extremely difficult for anyone suffering with arthritis; but she found it was quite worth it.

On the way to the crypt one had to either climb the stairs or walk up the ramp which passed by the crown of Our Lady. Since Carol couldn't do the stairs, she walked with great pain up the ramp, stopping to pray to Our Lady as she passed by the crown. Lourdes closes in mid-October for the winter and so on their last day, it was mostly just their pilgrimage group that was present.

Carol didn't think she could put into words the pain and trouble she was in on that last day. She couldn't even cut her meat at lunch. All the wheelchairs had to be returned to the hospital that day, so she and Margaret set off to bring hers back. She shared with Margaret her concern over being able to return on the plane. Carol feared that she would have to stay at one of the hospitals on the grounds. How would she ever explain to her family back home, she thought? Margaret helped her to get to Jesus in the crypt where she cried and stayed with Jesus for about half-hour. The coldness of the crypt chilled her body which became so stiff and was in much pain as she walked down to the baths and sat outside with the other women as the volunteers were about half-hour late in opening the baths. When the time came for her to go in, she couldn't move, so the volunteers put her in a wheelchair, took her inside, prepared her to enter the baths, wrapped a blue cloak around her, and sat her in a corner in order to wait her turn. She sat alone, crying by herself, knowing she was not leaving Lourdes. And so she asked our Blessed Mother to please get her home, that's all, and then do with her what-ever she needed to do. Carol placed herself totally in Our Lady's hands.

The volunteers picked her up and placed all of her in the bath water which was so cold it took her breath away! When she got up she was completely dry and walked out of the baths on her own!! Her friend Margaret was waiting for her outside. When she saw Carol, she asked what happened inside, as she no longer had any sign of pain on her face or in her eyes. Carol felt afraid, not understanding what truly happened, and asked Margaret not to tell anyone. She needed time to discern what was happening to her.

They left to go back to the hotel to get

their bags as they were leaving once again for Dublin to fly home from there the next day. Carol picked up her suitcase and walked down a flight of stairs with it. Her insides were so filled with excitement that she actually could do this! Margaret kept her word and said nothing. Away they flew; and in the early morning when it was still dark, they went to church. Carol kept looking at her feet as she was actually keeping up with everyone! It was wonderful! At Mass she thanked Our Lady so much for allowing her to go home, as at this time, she believed this was what our Mother was doing for her. Margaret and she spent the rest of the morning shopping and that afternoon boarded their plane for home.

On the plane, one of their friends came over to talk with them. As she was standing above Carol, she placed her hands on her right shoulder, kind of leaning on her in a way, which filled Carol's heart with joy, because, not only did she not feel any pain, but it felt good!! In response to this, she sat up and without even thinking about it, placed her knees under her. She hadn't been able to sit like this for years! SHE KNEW!!! She knew she was cured at Lourdes!!

Trying to hold back her tears, she saw Fr.

Charest walking towards her and sitting next to her, he asked her what had happened. Margaret told him something about it. Carol told Father everything she knew and believed, but asked him not to tell anyone until she saw her doctor in two weeks. She wanted to let the doctor tell her what he thought. Then, she told Father, she would call him immediately. Father agreed.

Arriving back home at JFK in New York, Carol walked through immigration with two, one-pound plastic bottles of Lourdes water. Walking quickly, and carrying her purse and the bottles, she soon came to where her family was waiting for her. She kissed them all, and excitedly anticipated a reaction from them upon seeing her walking, but no one said a word, especially her husband, Bob. When she couldn't hold it in anymore, she stopped in the middle of the road as they were going across to the parking area. "Don't you see anything different about me or how I look?" Bob turned to her and said, "I don't need to ask, when I saw you coming out of the door, I knew something happened right away, but I was afraid to ask." They talked about it all the way home, and for quite a few days after, but once again, it wasn't until she went to her doctor, then and there, that they definitely knew.

And so, Carol kept her appointment with her doctor. He had a Jewish intern with him that day. She lay on the table very quietly, being afraid she would blurt it all out. Her doctor began explaining to the intern the different nodules and areas where the joints were so badly attacked and disfigured, but the intern just looked at him with a questioning look on his face, as he could not see anywhere on her body as to what her doctor was talking about.

Finally her doctor, frustrated as could be, since he knew what Carol had, stood back and replied with his hands on his hips, "I don't understand what is going on here. I know my patient's condition and what it has done to her." (He could not find any evidence of her psoriasis arthritis). At this point Carol looked up at him and asked, "Aren't you going to ask me about my trip to Lourdes?" With that her doctor exclaimed, "You were cured at Lourdes!" "This explains why there are no nodules or joint damage!" He then proceeded to write across her chart with a broad smile on his face, "Cured at Lourdes." Carol started crying and her doctor was filled with excitement and happiness at seeing such a miraculous change in Carol.

Needless to say she called Fr. Charest

right away. In the following spring, Father came for a visit. He asked if he could take a picture of Carol's husband, Bob and one of her, and they both said yes. Father didn't explain why nor did they ask why. Upon his next visit, while they all sat on their back porch, Father showed them a Montfort magazine telling them there was an article in it about their pilgrimage and then he handed it to her. She opened to the page where there was a picture of Carol that Father had taken, with the whole story of her cure. Tears were shed, and together they celebrated all over again all that had happened. As far as Carol can remember, the year was 1979.

The following year, Carol, Bob and their three boys went to Lourdes where she consecrated all of them to our Blessed Mother. As she watched the Candlelight procession of the sick, with so many people on stretchers and in wheelchairs, she saw herself, and in that moment understood the love and mercy of Jesus and Mary towards her. Not only was her prayer answered to arrive home safely, but the terrible condition she had was taken away from her. At first she kept asking, "Why me?" Then God helped her understand that it was His gift to her, unworthy of it as she was. He was her God, her Creator and could do with her as it pleased Him. How she thanked God for the love and mercy He gave her!!

Carol wanted to do something special for Our Lady, as she was the one who interceded for her and gained the blessings she received from her Son. Since they began their pilgrimage on October 7th, which is the feast of Our Lady of the Rosary, Carol knew how much it would please our Mother Mary to have a living candlelight Rosary each year to honor her. And so began many years of living rosaries of petition in her parish church to help those who have been away from Our Lord to come back to Jesus through our Blessed Mother's heartfelt prayers.

Our Lady invites us to Lourdes to assist us in our conversion from our sinful ways and to obtain for us much peace from her Son, Our Lord and Savior Jesus Christ.

Carol believes she was blessed at Lourdes by Our Lady by helping her to face her pride. She was also given the additional gift of being cured of her arthritis for which she is profoundly grateful.

The Vision at Knock, Ireland

Outdoor grotto and shrine where Our Lady
appeared to St. Bernadette

189

THE SACRED HEART OF JESUS

A number of years ago there was a flyer in our Sunday bulletin that featured an account of a parishioner, a woman named Gerry, who witnessed to the blessings of the Enthronement of the Sacred Heart of Jesus in the family. The following narrative tells much of her story.

This young mother related that she had discovered the Sacred Heart quite by accident. A very kind, elderly woman gave her a pin of the Sacred Heart as a gift for doing her a small favor. Gerry didn't really want the gift, but she knew that this particular woman had great devotion to the Sacred Heart, so she just thanked her and thoughtlessly put the pin in her handbag. She didn't think about it much, unless she was shuffling through her bag looking for something, and happened to accidentally get stuck by the small pin on the back of it. In fact she admitted she really didn't want the pin at all, but was afraid if she ran into the woman who gave it to her she might be hurt if she learned that Gerry didn't have the pin with her. Rather than take the chance of offending her, she begrudgingly held onto it, *just in case.*

At this particular time, Gerry was going

through an extraordinarily dark period in her life. She was recovering from a rare, experimental brain surgery. She had just spent the previous ten years flat on her back suffering from what she felt was an incurable brain disorder. She stated that her illness was not an individual disease, but one that had devastated her entire family as well, her husband and two small children. She did not know at this point if her surgery had been successful. It can take, she was told, anywhere from three to twelve months to take effect. After six months of showing no improvement, her husband, who had tirelessly and unselfishly, taken care of her and their two young children all those years, had given up all hope of her recovery. In desperation, one day he packed a bag and walked out. She knew at this point she had only one option, "Let go and let God."

She slowly found the courage to get out of bed every day and started going to morning Mass to beg God to help her find a way out of what she called a nightmare. Her brain surgery still showed very little, if any, signs of success. Both her children as well as she were severely depressed. She was too incapacitated to work, and there was almost no money left to even put food on the table. She felt that she had little choice other than to file for divorce.

One day as she was leaving the church, she came across a bookmark that included *The Twelve Promises of the Sacred Heart.* She became mesmerized by the second promise on the list, "I will give peace in their families." At this point, she was desperate for anything that would give her any hope at all and knew that what she and the children truly needed was some peace. During this same time period, by what she thought was a strange coincidence or Divine intervention, the church was holding its first meeting on the Enthronement of the Sacred Heart. She made up her mind that she had to be there to find out what she could about the strong pull she was experiencing after she read the promises of Our Lord. Gerry felt truly inspired by what she heard at the meeting and wasted no time in setting up an altar in her home. She encouraged the children to join her in saying nightly prayers together to ask the Sacred Heart to restore their home to some kind of peace and sanity. And the most wonderful thing is, He did.

In almost no time at all, things began to happen. With each new day she could feel herself gradually getting healthier and better able to function. Likewise her children seemed happier and started doing better in school. She was even able to start putting her home, which had been neglected for years, back together. Slowly she began to exercise again and lost eighty pounds of the over one hundred pounds she had gained. She also returned to college after a twenty year absence and started pursuing a degree. She knew at this point that this was not a coincidence, but the graces of the Sacred Heart coming to them in gratitude for her and her children's devotion to Him.

Gerry went on to receive even more blessings, and was eventually able to make a full recovery. Amazingly, after follow-up research evaluation, she was diagnosed with the best results of anyone who had been given this very rare experimental brain surgery. At this point, her children were not only doing well, they were thriving! She finished college, graduating Summa Cum Laude. And to her surprise, two years after her husband left her and one month before signing the final divorce papers, her husband came to her and told her he felt that God was calling him to go back home.

While reluctant at first to take him back, Gerry felt in her heart that it was God's will that they should be reunited. They went through a program offered by the Catholic Church for troubled marriages called "Retrouvaille," meaning "Rediscovery," which greatly helped them to heal their devastated relationship.

After her husband's return the family began to pray together, asking the Sacred Heart of Jesus to continue to bless them and thanking Him for keeping His promise of peace in their home. "And remember," Gerry wrote, "This is only one of the promises that Jesus made, there are eleven others!"

The flyer in our bulletin ended with this statement by Gerry, "Today, people are willing to try just about anything to make their lives and the lives of their families better. They invest so much time and energy into chasing the "good life." They feel that by going to the best schools, driving the fastest cars, having the nicest homes, earning the highest incomes, having the most influential friends, and making the right investments that it will give them "the wonderful life", and these things probably will give them short term gratification. But if you are looking for the wonderful life, for the rest of your life, then invest a few minutes of each day in the Sacred Heart and you really will have a wonderful life, not only in this world, but, more importantly, in the next."

The Twelve Promises of the Sacred Heart

1. *I will give them all the graces necessary for their state in life.*
2. *I will give peace in their families.*
3. *I will console them in all their troubles.*
4. *They will find in My Heart an assured refuge during life and especially at the hour of death.*
5. *I will pour abundant blessings on all their undertakings.*
6. *Sinners shall find in My Heart the source and infinite ocean of mercy.*
7. *Lukewarm souls will become fervent.*
8. *Fervent souls will speedily rise to great perfection.*
9. *I will bless the homes in which the image of My Sacred Heart shall be exposed and honored.*
10. *I will give to priests the power to touch the most hardened hearts.*
11. *Those who propagate this devotion will have their names written in My Heart, and they will never be effaced.*
12. *The all-powerful love of My Heart will grant to all those who shall receive*

Communion on the First Friday of nine consecutive months the grace of final repentance; they shall not die under My displeasure, nor without receiving their Sacraments; My Heart shall be their assured refuge at that last hour.

These promises were revealed to Sister Margaret Mary Alacoque, a Visitation nun in France, by Our Lord Jesus, in the year of 1675. He confided to her the mission to establish devotion to His Sacred Heart. Jesus made known to her His ardent desire to be loved by men. He revealed to her His Heart which has loved men so much, and is so little loved in return. "Through you My Divine Heart wishes to spread its love everywhere on earth." He made known to her the above promises to those who would respond to His love and make an effort to love Him in return. He also told Sister Margaret Mary that He desired the faithful to come to the foot of the altar. He promised that there great graces would be poured out from His Sacred Heart.

Pope Benedict XV canonized Sister Margaret Mary Alacoque a saint in 1920.

SAINT JUDE, SAINT OF THE IMPOSSIBLE

Our son Jack had been looking for a job unsuccessfully. Then one day I said, "Jack, tomorrow October 28, is the feast of St. Jude, Saint of the Impossible. Why not come to the nine o'clock Mass with me and pray that he'll help you find a job." To my surprise he decided to go. He always went to Mass on Sundays but not during the week. Within one week he had two job offers! He took the one with a brokerage firm and has been a successful bond salesman for many years. Thank you, St. Jude, for answering our prayers.

St. Jude has been forgotten by many, because people mistake him for the traitor, Judas Iscariot. St. Jude, Thaddeus, as he is called in the gospels by Matthew and Mark, was one of the twelve apostles. He is often invoked by the faithful in difficult or hopeless cases.

~~~~~~~~~~

One day Kathy, a good friend of mine, called to tell me how concerned she was about her friend Jane's husband, Jim, who was in the hospital and was terminally ill. He was born and raised Catholic, but had been away from the church for many years and had told his wife not to call a priest.

I said to Kathy, "Let's start a novena, (nine days of prayer) for your friend Jim. I'll make a novena to Saint Jude, Saint of the Impossible, and you make a novena to whomever you would like." Kathy agreed, and we both began either that day or the next. I also advised my friend to call the priest chaplain of the hospital where Jim was a patient, describe the circumstances of Jim and his health and ask the chaplain to visit their friend to see what he could do.

The next time Kathy and her husband Tom went to the hospital to see Jim, his wife Jane was also there. Jim barked at Tom, "Did you call a priest to ask him to come and see me?" Tom was able to answer truthfully, "No" (because it was Kathy who had called the priest)!!

Unfortunately, Father was unable to move Jim's heart at that time; at least that's how it appeared. But in a couple of weeks, lo and behold, Jim himself asked for the priest to come back and pay him another visit. Jim made his confession, received Holy Communion, was anointed, and died peacefully within the next couple of days. How beautifully the saints answer our prayers! Thanks be to God for His wondrous, merciful love!

We hope these stories inspire all who read them to pray often for the dying, especially for those who are not ready to meet their Maker.

"For you, O Lord, are good and forgiving, abounding in kindness to all who call upon you."
(Psalm 86:5)

~~~~~~~~~

My husband Ed, because of his addiction to cigarettes, was one of those impossible cases. How often he tried to give up smoking, but to no avail. It started out quite innocently in his adult life. A friend of his, Jim, with whom he rode on the train to New York, asked him on their way to work, if he would like a cigarette. He put it this way, "keep me company" as he offered it to him. Before he knew it, having that cigarette was becoming a habit, one on the train, and then one on the ferry with his friend. When Jim went on vacation, Ed missed the cigarette and decided to buy a pack of his own. That was the beginning of the end! He was hooked! Those were the days before anyone realized smoking could be such a health hazard. And cigarettes were a lot cheaper then.

Eventually, after many years of smoking, Ed tried to give it up. He figured the best time would be when we were on vacation, where he wouldn't have the stress of work. Of course he was more irritable than relaxed while we were away, because of the difficulty involved for an avid smoker to give up the habit. He even resorted to removing someone else's butts in the sand by the elevator at our timeshare in order to have a little puff. When one of our daughters heard this she was horrified and reprimanded him vehemently.

Every Friday after work, before Ed got on the train at Grand Central Station to go home, he paid a visit to St. Agnes Church nearby where they had exposition of the Blessed Sacrament, a beautiful shrine to Our Lady of Lourdes, and other statues in memory of the saints including St. Theresa, St. Patrick, St. Lucy, and St. Jude. After praying his Rosary in front of the Blessed Sacrament, Ed made his rounds to Our Lady's Shrine and the other saints mentioned, asking their help in giving up cigarettes. He knew how impossible a case he was, so he prayed especially to St. Jude. At times he also took advantage of going to the Sacrament of Reconciliation (confession) which is regularly offered daily at St. Agnes and a number of other Catholic Churches in New York City.

Ed was an impossible case. He even made a deal with me. If I lost weight and went down to 125 pounds, (that meant losing about twenty pounds at the time), he would give up smoking, or so he said. I did, and he didn't! When I reached my goal, he gave up smoking-- for one day! I would like to say I was a little annoyed but that wouldn't be exactly correct.

One summer we were having work done in the basement of our home when he was trying to give up smoking. Guess what? After the workmen left he went down to the basement and found on the floor the flattened butts put out by the men. Ed would round them out and smoke them all! But he never gave up praying.

Finally, one day he tried again, and that was it, he stopped smoking! We were at a neighborhood gathering of friends, a few months later in January, and someone noticed that Ed wasn't smoking and asked, "Ed, when did you give up smoking?" Ed answered, "My last cigarette was October 28th." I could hardly believe what I was hearing, because I didn't realize that was the day he gave them up. I said, "Ed, that's the feast of St. Jude, Saint of the Impossible!" What a gift! How grateful we were to St. Jude who helps make what seems impossible, possible.

Prayer to St. Jude, Saint of the Impossible

Most holy Apostle St. Jude, faithful servant and friend of Jesus, the name of the traitor who delivered your Divine Master into the hands of his enemies has caused you to be forgotten by many, but the Church honors and invokes you universally as the patron of hopeless cases and of things despaired of. Pray for me who am so miserable. Make use I implore you, of that particular privilege accorded to you to bring visible and speedy help where help is almost despaired of. Come to my assistance in this great need that I may receive the consolation and succor of heaven in all my necessities, tribulations and sufferings particularly (here mention your request) and that I may bless God with you and all the elect forever. I promise you,

O blessed St. Jude to be ever mindful of this great favor, and I will never cease to honor you as my special and powerful patron and to do all in my power to bring honor and devotion to you. Amen.

Our 60th Wedding Anniversary

With our children, from left: Jack, Kerry,
Elizabeth, Jackie, Ed, Debbie, Mary Therese, Diane

ANOTHER ANSWER TO PRAYER

Around the time Ed and I were introduced to the Marriage Encounter Weekend I read an article in the newspaper about "Recovery Inc." and I thought it might be helpful. I decided to attend one of their meetings held weekly in a room at the Episcopal Church in our area. The Recovery program was also held each week on another day in a room at one of the Roman Catholic Churches in the vicinity, which was where I went most of the time because the meeting was held in the evening and that was more convenient for me.

Recovery Inc., now known as Recovery International, was set up in 1937 by Dr. Abraham Low, a psychiatrist, to help people who have had nervous breakdowns to become well again. Many others who have not had breakdowns have also been helped by attending the meetings. There is no fee to attend. A free will donation bag is passed. No one knows the amount, if any, that anyone else has given. Recovery is a self-help will training program.

At my first meeting I started to wonder why I had come. Thank God I never had a nervous breakdown or needed to visit a psychologist or other mental health physician. But as I sat there listening to the people who came and shared how they used the tools they learned in Recovery, with the help of a trained leader, I realized that the program could help me to become more patient and calm, which it did. I went to the meetings for about a year and a half until the leader asked me, "Jackie, do you really need Recovery?" Except for a rare occasion that was my last meeting.

I shared the benefits of Recovery with a number of friends. Most of them found the program to be of great help and continued attending the meetings. An aunt, who had suffered a breakdown and was hospitalized, decided to try Recovery on my recommendation when she came home. She told me Recovery was a tremendous help to her. She never had to be hospitalized again.

One of my friends told me that her husband was very concerned about her since he often found her crying even though she tried to hide her tears from him. She had suffered from depression for so many years. She told me she even contemplated suicide but knew if she expected her son, who was having difficulties, to rise above them and turn out well, she couldn't possibly give into that temptation which was also against her religious convictions.

She decided to go to a Recovery meeting and was immediately encouraged. She told her husband that she finally found people like her and asked him never to stand in her way of attending the meetings. She also asked him to encourage her to keep on going as that would mean a lot to her. She made a tremendous recovery and eventually she, with her husband, were a great example to others with their apostolic endeavors.

Dr. Low always stated that Recovery does not replace the doctor. It can be a great addition to medical help for those suffering from mental illness. He also stated, "There is no hopeless case."

At one point my husband Ed was getting very upset at work. He was getting so uptight I was afraid he was going to have a breakdown. I begged him to go to Recovery. He didn't want to. I told him, "Quit the job, we'll sell the house, and move to an apartment." Thank God, he decided to go to Recovery. He went for about six months. It helped him to calm down, to deal with the frustrations of the job, and continue working for the same firm until he retired.

Our children also benefited because I often shared with them the tools I learned, e.g. "temper is a luxury I cannot afford," (a situation) is "distressing but not dangerous," (relating to the trivialities of everyday life). What fun it was to hear one of our daughters at the age of four or five say, "It's distressing but not dangerous," when something unexpected happened.

I thought many of the tools could be related to something Our Lord Jesus or Holy Scripture teaches us. For example, "I'll willingly bear the discomfort of my feelings for a higher motive, if for no other reason than my own mental health," (which, to me, contributes to peace of mind and soul). Jesus said, *"Come to me, all you who labor and are burdened, and I will give you rest. Take my yoke upon you, and learn from me, for I am meek and humble of heart; and you will find rest for your selves. For my yoke is easy, and my burden light."* (Matthew 11:28-30.) Recovery says, "There is no impulse that cannot be controlled." Jesus said, **"Ask and it will be given to you…"** (Matthew 7:7.) Another helpful tool is, "I can, if I care to (bear the discomfort of my feelings for a higher motive, etc.)," while doing a necessary chore one dislikes doing.

Recovery meetings have helped many to regain their equilibrium and put into practice the tenets of their faith. I truly felt that the Holy Spirit answered my prayers years ago by leading us to the Marriage Encounter weekend and the Recovery program.

Note: Anyone interested in learning more about Recovery can go on line for more information at: www.recoveryinternational.org or call: 1-866-221-0302.

A MOTHER'S DAY GIFT

Our family lived for about twenty-four years in a house that was built in the early 1900s. It was heated by steam heat through radiators that were covered with metal and wood radiator covers. The metal part on the front and sides had little attractive holes in it, in order to let the heat through. One day as I went into our guest room, I placed the back of my left hand on the front cover of the radiator to see if the heat was coming up since the room felt a little cool. Out popped the diamond from my ring as I tried to remove my hand. One of the small metal holes in the radiator cover plucked the diamond right out of my ring! I couldn't believe it!

Okay, I figured I'd find it as soon as I bent down and looked for it. No way! The carpet in the room was an unusually high shag rug. I took off the radiator cover, and searched all over, under the radiator, and all around it, for about a radius of three or four feet. I could not find my diamond no matter how hard I looked. I finally took out the vacuum cleaner, removed the dust bag and put a new one inside so that I could hopefully vacuum the diamond up into the new bag. No success. My husband helped me search for it and we both spent a long time combing through the pile of the rug, moving the thick threads this way and that, but to no avail. I knew it was there; we just could *not* find it.

A couple of months later, Mother's Day weekend was coming up and we invited Ed's mother to come to spend the day with us and the family, and to stay overnight. Around 10:00 p.m. or so, being tired after a long day, I told Ed and his mother I was going up to bed. As I approached my bedroom I thought I should go and turn on the light in the guest room for Ed's mother to make it easier for her to see where she was going. As awful as it sounds, somehow I didn't feel like turning around to do that. But before I entered my room I decided to go back, knowing that would be the loving thing to do, and went down the hall to the guest room to turn the light on for her. The lamp was on a night table on the other side of the bed. As I turned around to leave the room, a sparkle on the rug caught my eye! Could that be my diamond?! I went over to the sparkle and sure enough, as little as my diamond was, there it was sitting right side up on top of the shag rug! I didn't touch it! Instead I went barreling down the stairs to tell Ed and his Mom to come upstairs; I wanted to show them something. Somewhat reluctantly they came up without my telling them what it was I wanted them to see. When they arrived in the room I stood quietly and pointed to the diamond. How it sparkled! They couldn't get over it! The three of us rejoiced! What a Mother's Day gift! Thanks be to God!

OUR LADY OF GUADALUPE

The Basilica of Our Lady of Guadalupe in Mexico City is the most visited Catholic pilgrimage site in the world. In 1983, in celebration of our 30th wedding anniversary, my husband and I decided to go on vacation to Mexico, and the highlight of our trip was our visit to the Shrine of Our Lady of Guadalupe in Mexico City. Inside the Shrine displayed on one of the walls is the tilma (cloak), with a miraculous image of our Blessed Mother on it, worn by Juan Diego, a poor Aztec Indian to whom our Blessed Mother appeared almost 500 years ago.

The taxi we were in on the way to the Basilica had to stop for a red light. As we stopped, a young woman came up to our window to offer for sale a dozen roses to bring inside. As I looked for a pleasing amount to give to the woman in exchange for the roses the cab driver raised his voice and said insistently, "Give her a dollar!" How many times whenever I've thought of the incident have I regretted listening to him! As I gave her the dollar which the woman accepted as she gave me the roses, the sad look on her face makes me feel regretful about my paying attention to the driver whenever that memory comes back to me. He was anxious to get going since the light had turned green.

As we approached the Basilica we saw a number of pilgrims on their knees prayerfully and humbly advancing towards the entrance. Once inside I saw the altar steps were full of roses brought by the people in veneration of Our Lord and His Blessed Mother. I was so very pleased to place ours there also and noticed that I was able to put the red roses I had right next to a dozen white and a dozen pink ones which made me think of the Joyful, Sorrowful and the Glorious Mysteries of the rosary. (In the year 2002 Pope John Paul II wrote his Apostolic Letter, Rosarium Virginis Mariae and added the Luminous Mysteries which are: The Baptism in the Jordan, The Wedding at Cana, The Proclamation of the Kingdom, The Transfiguration and The Institution of the Eucharist.)

It was a blessing to be present at the Holy Sacrifice of the Mass in the Basilica of Our Lady of Guadalupe. The miraculous image can be seen by all who visit the Shrine. During our visit we also had the advantage to go up to a moving platform that took the visitors slowly past the tilma so the image could be seen ever so much better. Many miracles have occurred through the veneration of the tilma; so many that the Shrine has stopped keeping a record of them. How did this all come about?

When Juan Diego was walking by the hill of Tepeyac on December 9, 1531, he heard beautiful music and saw a radiant young woman. She spoke to him in his native tongue and told him her name was Mary, the Mother of the one true God and Mother of all mankind. She asked Juan to go to the Bishop to tell him that she requested a Church be built there on that site.

Juan Diego obeyed Our Lady and traveled to see the Bishop to tell him of her request. The Bishop initially didn't believe Juan, but told him when Juan went to see him a second time at Our Lady's request, to ask the Lady for a sign that what Juan was telling him was true. Our Lady consented to give Juan a sign for the Bishop, however on that day Juan was taking care of his uncle who became seriously ill. Juan tried to avoid meeting with Our Lady so he could fetch a priest to prepare his uncle for his death. On his way to get a priest for his uncle, Our Lady appeared to Juan, told him his uncle had recovered and that he should gather some roses that were growing on the top of the hill to bring to the Bishop. Even though it was December and not the season for roses, when Juan looked where Our Lady told him, and he saw beautiful roses blooming, native to the Bishop's homeland in Spain, (Castilian roses, which the Bishop desired), which he cut and brought to her. She arranged them in his tilma and off he went to visit the Bishop once more. It was December 12th. (On December 13th Juan's uncle told him that Our Lady visited him also and he regained his health!)

When Juan arrived to see the Bishop and opened his tilma the roses fell out and all present fell to their knees as they gazed on the Miraculous Image of Our Lady in full color that was on the inside of Juan's tilma. This image has remained intact for almost 500 years!! It proclaimed to the Aztec Indians by its content that the Spanish Missionaries were teaching the truth and millions of Aztec Indians were converted to the Catholic Faith in a short time and stopped their practice of sacrificing humans, including children, to their pagan gods. Juan Diego and his wife Maria Lucia had already converted to Catholicism soon after the Spanish Missionaries arrived in Mexico.

Juan's tilma was made of cactus fiber that should have disintegrated within several years. The image of the Blessed Virgin Mary on the cloth is surrounded by rays of sunlight with a crescent of the moon under her feet. The colors on the tilma have been proven not to be from any paint known to mankind. The black tassels tied high on her waist denote pregnancy to the Aztec culture. It is the only apparition where Our Lady left a miraculous image of herself where the Madonna appears pregnant with child. Upon microscopic examination in the last century, of the eyes on the tilma, the pupils showed the reflection of the Bishop and those present in the room when Juan opened his tilma! Because the image portrays Our Lady pregnant with child, she is called Patroness of the Unborn and is venerated by the Pro-Life Movement.

Our Lady of Guadalupe to Juan Diego, 1531:

"Listen. Put it into your heart my smallest child, that the thing that frightened you, the thing that afflicted you is nothing: Do not let it disturb you...Am I not here, I who am your mother? Are you not under my shadow and protection? Am I not the source of your joy? Are you not in the hollow of my mantle, in the crossing of my arms? Do you need something more?"

To obtain a card of Our Lady of Guadalupe with these words of Our Lady on the back, contact:

Association of Marian Helpers, Stockbridge, MA 01263 or call 800-462-7426.

    ✧ *Pope Pius X proclaimed Our Lady of Guadalupe the Patron of Latin America in 1910.*
    ✧ *Pope Pius X1 declared her "Heavenly Patroness of the Philippines" in 1935.*
    ✧ *Pope Pius XII gave her the title, "Queen of Mexico and Empress of the Americas" in 1945, and "Patroness of the Americas" in 1946.*
    ✧ *Pope John Paul II canonized Juan Diego a saint on July 31, 2002. His feast day is December 9th.*

Our Lady of Guadalupe

For more information on Our Lady of Guadalupe and also on the Missionary Image of Our Lady of Guadalupe (an exact photographic replica of the original image) and its many visitations throughout the United States and the world, there is a book: "Our Lady of Guadalupe Hope for the World" by Dan Lynch.

Available at John Paul Press, 144 Sheldon Road, St. Albans, VT 05478, or 802-524-5350. e-mail: JKMI@JKMI.com; www.JKMI.com

ST. RAPHAEL, THE ARCHANGEL

A number of years ago I was invited to a meeting of women at the home of Cathy. One of the women present named Ann, told this amazing story. Ann, who was a widow, had a great devotion to St. Raphael, the patron of travelers. She often prayed to this angel, especially when she was traveling. One day while she was driving south on the Hutchinson River Parkway in N.Y., her car started to overheat so she pulled over onto the shoulder of the road, unsure of what she was going to do next. This happened before the prevalent use of cell phones.

There were some houses in the area, close to the parkway. Ann noticed a woman in the distance in her back yard watering her flowers, but Ann had no container in the car in order to bring it to the woman to ask her for some water. As she was thinking over her problem, all of a sudden another car pulled up behind her. Two men in business suits approached and asked if she needed any help. When she told them her problem, they offered to go to obtain some water for her from the woman since they had an empty can in their car. The men said that they were at a business meeting in White Plains. She noticed one of them had a name tag on the lapel of his suit. She thought the name was rather unusual. It was Azariah.

There was a small stream near the shoulder of the road that the men had to walk through to get to the woman's yard. They removed their shoes and socks and walked through the stream to ask the woman for water for our friend's car. She was very gracious and let them fill their container. They then came back to Ann's car and filled the water receptacle. Ann noticed how strange it was that they both walked through the stream and the bottom of their trousers weren't the least bit wet. She thanked the men for helping her and went on her way back home.

When she arrived at her apartment, in thanksgiving to St. Raphael for sending her some help when she needed it, she decided to open her Bible and reread the story of Tobit, his son Tobias, and St. Raphael. When she came to the part where Tobias met an admirable young man who offered to be his guide to Rages, a city of the Medes to collect a debt due his father Tobit, she was astonished to read that the guide gave his name as "Azariah," who later revealed himself as

St. Raphael! We can all imagine how amazed Ann was when she read that name!

She had completely forgotten that St. Raphael called himself Azariah when he first came to Tobias. It was only after his mission was completed that he revealed himself.

"I am Raphael, one of the seven angels who stand and serve before the Glory of the Lord."
(Tobit 12:15)

Prayer to St. Raphael

Blessed St. Raphael, Archangel, we beseech thee to help us in all our needs and trials of this life, as thou, through the power of God, didst restore sight and give guidance to young Tobit. We humbly seek thine aid and intercession, that our souls may be healed, our bodies protected from all ills, and through divine grace we may be made fit to dwell in the eternal Glory of God in heaven. Amen.

MEDJUGORJE

In 1989 there was an announcement in our parish bulletin that one of our priests, Fr. Patrick Walsh, S.M.A., was going on pilgrimage to Medjugorje, a small village in Bosnia-Herzegovina, in the former Yugoslavia where the Blessed Virgin Mary is said to have been appearing every day since June 24, 1981, to six young people. Father was inviting anyone who was interested to join him on this pilgrimage. How excited I was when my husband agreed to my going! My husband's mother, Betty, her friend Sophie, and our daughter Elizabeth, also expressed a desire to go and so we all joined the group. It was a long trip overseas but ever so worthwhile.

Father warned us ahead of time that there could be many sacrifices asked of us during this trip. He pointed out the possible delays in plane schedules and the difficulty that might arise connecting planes when there was a delay. Someone's luggage might be lost, but hopefully returned in a couple of days, etc. He asked us to endure everything in a good spirit, in a spirit of sacrifice, and to offer it up for our own spiritual benefit and for that of others. He was right! I recall one woman whose luggage did not come off the plane when it was supposed to and she had to borrow some clothes until her suitcase arrived a couple of days later.

How beautiful was the bus ride through the country once we got off the plane! We saw a magnificent waterfall cascading into a lake, and gorgeous hills and valleys on our way to Medjugorje. We were so happy when we finally arrived in the little village where so many people from all over the world were coming together to be present at Our Lady's apparitions.

Our first big mishap was when my mother-in-law fell down a number of stairs that approached the house where we were staying for the next five days. The owner of the home was so solicitous with Mom, and very upset that she got hurt. He helped her into the house, sat her down, and offered her a glass of brandy. He brought her some ice to put on her knees to help prevent further swelling since they had already started to puff up. Her knees got all black and blue and remained that way during our stay, but thank God nothing was broken and she was able to join us for just about everything that was planned except for climbing Cross Mountain.

At that time, in 1989, our Blessed Mother

was appearing to the visionaries in the choir loft of the parish church of St. James every evening at 6:40 p.m. And prior to that time, at 6:00 p.m. the people in great numbers, would arrive inside the church to pray with the priest, a Franciscan, who would lead the people in the rosary in preparation for Our Lady's visit.

It was amazing how quickly the church was filled with people from so many different countries. Every seat was taken. Many brought small collapsible seats so they could sit in the aisles. The rest of the people remained standing. There was a great, prayerful reverence throughout the church. After the five Joyful Mysteries were recited, Father would begin the Sorrowful Mysteries and when the time approached for our Blessed Mother's visitation to the children, Father gave the people time for quiet prayer before 6:40 p.m. arrived.

I remember kneeling and praying quietly within myself. At one point I glanced at my watch and noticed it was 6:38 p.m. Soon after that, all of a sudden I felt a tremendous peace coming down through the church on my upper left. I could actually feel the peace descending upon and filling me so completely that my arms just dropped to my side and I knew our Blessed

Mother was there.

I was full of gratitude since I didn't expect or ask for any special experience when I came to Medjugorje. I wasn't looking to see Our Lady, I knew I wasn't worthy of that, I just wanted to be there when she came to visit the children. Of course I prayed with all my heart to her, and when I felt again like myself, I lifted up my arm and looked at my watch. It was 6:42 p.m.!! The visionaries have said that she usually appears for two or three minutes! How grateful I was to have experienced her presence in the church!! What a tremendous gift from God!! I was filled with joy!

Soon Father began to finish the rest of the rosary and holy Mass was celebrated at 7:00 o'clock. I believe after the Mass we had our third rosary, the Glorious Mysteries, and then the priest gave the people a very special blessing with a crucifix. Afterward, at nine o'clock we had dinner at the home of the family we were staying with. How good they were to us! They welcomed us warmly and treated us as very special guests.

Holy Mass is offered in a number of languages. The Mass in English was at 10:00 a.m. The Mass at 7:00 p.m. was in Croatian, the language of the people who live in the village. How beautiful it was to hear the people singing Ave, Ave, Ave, Maria between each of the mysteries, as the rosary was being prayed before and after Mass! This was one part where everyone in the church was singing in the same tongue!

Confessions are heard in a variety of languages. Confessionals were set up outside the church and the priest hearing confessionals would hang a sign up as to what language he spoke. So very many people took advantage of this great opportunity to reconcile themselves with God and 'begin again.' Our Blessed Mother is never wanting in giving us her help whenever we ask for it. She encourages us, through the visionaries, to go to confession at least once a month, more if we need to, (she knows human nature). The Sacrament of Reconciliation, (Confession), is an important part of a Catholic pilgrimage, in order to receive the most spiritual benefits, graces, and blessings that are being offered to us from our good Lord. He sees our efforts and is never outdone in generosity. What peace a good confession brings!

"On the evening of that first day of the week,

when the doors were locked, where the
disciples were for fear of the Jews, Jesus came
and stood in their midst and said to them,
'Peace be with you.' When he had said this, he
showed them his hands and his side. The
disciples rejoiced when they saw the Lord.
[Jesus] said to them again, 'Peace be with you.
As the Father has sent me, so I send you.'
And when he had said this, he breathed on
them and said to them, 'Receive the holy
Spirit. Whose sins you forgive are forgiven
them; and whose sins you retain are
retained.'"
(John 20:19-23)

Before I left for this first trip to Medjugorje in 1989, I asked some relatives and friends if they would like me to bring any prayer intentions with me. The pastor in our small summer parish in the Catskills made an announcement at Sunday Mass that I was going over there and let the people who wanted to write their intentions on a piece of paper for me to bring with me. He also gave me some intentions of his own. I put everything in an envelope without looking at any of them and gave them to our chaplain for the pilgrimage. He put all the intentions in his suitcase, along with the other intentions that he had. How happy our group was when Father was invited into the choir loft, with the visionaries the second night we were in the church! When our Blessed Mother came that night, I felt lifted right out of myself. Again I was so grateful, and prayed with all my heart, soul, and mind.

The third day we made a trip to Dubrovnik which was about two hours away by bus. We saw the Church of St. Basil which had a special area where his relics are kept. Dubrovnik is on the Adriatic Sea, which is so beautiful to look at with its azure color, and this also was a special day. But when we got back we didn't arrive at the church until it was almost time for our Blessed Mother's visit. I really didn't feel her presence that evening. I was not in quiet prayer, in fact we were rushing in order to get back in time. I guess it shows how important it is to make time for prayer.

Father Walsh was asked to offer the Mass on the fourth day of our pilgrimage. When it came time to preach the homily, he told the most wonderful story that one of the pilgrims with our group had related to him. This woman was from Pennsylvania. She had a young son who had become very seriously ill and she was given no hope of his recovery by the doctors. Unfortunately, she and her husband had drifted away from their Catholic faith, but when a friend gave her a relic of St. John Neumann, she placed it on her son's pillow as he was lying in his hospital bed and she prayed with all her heart for his recovery. She and her husband were in the hospital waiting room, where they kept night vigil of their son. About midnight, they happened to notice a young boy, about twelve years old, pass the door of the room they were in, as he walked down the hall. The next time they went in to see how their son was doing, he was awake, and he told them a young boy had come to see him.

The next day the doctors found him so much improved they were all completely astonished! When those in charge heard about the young boy that came to see the sick child they made inquiries as to how he got into the hospital at midnight. The guard said he saw no one come into the hospital at that time. In fact, no one saw him enter or leave the hospital! In a couple of days their son was discharged.

The young couple decided to go to St. John Neumann's Shrine in Philadelphia to thank him for answering their prayers for the recovery of their son. Of course they brought their young boy with them. At the shrine there were different items from the saint's life. "That's the boy who came to see me!" their son exclaimed, pointing to a picture of St. John Neumann when he was twelve years old! It was also the same boy that the parents had seen in the hospital, walking past the waiting room!!

What a miracle, that God would allow one of his saints to appear as he was when he was twelve, to visit this little boy who was critically ill, and be his instrument in the boy's healing! When Father finished relating this true story, he asked the boy's mother, who was in the congregation for Mass, to come up so he could introduce her to those present. Everyone applauded and was so happy to hear of this great miracle of God!! The mother told us that the family came back to the practice of their Catholic faith.

Afterwards, back at the house where we were staying, Father told us that a number of people came to him for Confession after the Mass. Praise God!

~~~~~~~~~~

The second time I went to Medjugorje, I traveled with six women and Fr. Gérard J. Breault, O.M.V. It was during the war over there. My husband was willing to let me go, (he is not a worrier), but a few others expressed their concern for our safety. A day or two before we left, our son Jack called and asked me if I thought I really should go, considering the fighting that was going on over there. Our daughter Debbie also tried to talk me out of it.

The night before we left, before I started my Rosary, I prayed to our Blessed Mother. I asked her to please let me know if I should, or shouldn't, go on this trip. Now I don't ever expect an immediate answer to prayer. After I finished my rosary, I remembered I hadn't yet read a psalm that day, which was one of the prayers I prayed daily at that time, usually in the morning. After a prayer to the Holy Spirit, I would then open to a psalm at random. That night I opened to Psalm 121:

The LORD Our Guardian
A song of ascents.

***"I lift up my eyes toward the mountains; /
whence shall help come to me? / My help is***

from the LORD, / *who made heaven and earth.
/ May he not suffer your foot to slip; / may he
slumber not who guards you: Indeed he
neither slumbers nor sleeps, / the guardian of
Israel.*

The LORD *is your guardian; / the* LORD *is your
shade / he is beside you at your right hand.
The sun shall not harm you by day/ nor the
moon by night.*

The LORD *will guard you from all evil; / he
will guard your life. The* LORD *will guard
your coming and your going, / both now and
forever. "*

After I read this psalm I was filled with
joy and confidence. I immediately telephoned my
friend Mary and her twin sister Anne, to tell them
of my prayer and the psalm that the Holy Spirit
led me to. Mary and Anne are the only children
of their widowed mother, and naturally their
mother, whose name also was Mary, was worried
about their safety. We all rejoiced in the peace
that Psalm 121 gave us. On the following day, my
husband drove our priest friend, Fr. Breault and
me to Kennedy Airport where we were to meet

the rest of the group. On the way to the airport we decided to pray the Rosary. After a little while I noticed a very light, heavenly aroma in the car. I decided the scent must be an after-shave lotion that either our priest friend or my husband had applied.

All of a sudden, Fr. Breault said, "Hey, look at this!" The links that connected his rosary beads had turned a deep gold in color! Before this they were silver in color. Previously the Cross on the rosary was silver in color. Now either the Corpus or the background, I can't remember which, had turned gold in color. Our Blessed Mother's mantle on the medal on which is prayed the "Hail Holy Queen" had turned gold and a small part, covering her hair under the mantle, had remained silver! It was absolutely amazing! What a gift from heaven to encourage us even before we got on the plane!

Upon seeing Fr. Breault's rosary, everyone at the airport in our group was so edified and full of joy! The smile on the face of the mother of the twins, when she saw this sign from heaven, which brought her a great peace, meant a lot to all of us who couldn't help but notice it.

How different this pilgrimage was during the war, from the pilgrimage I made in 1989 during a time of peace. There were very few pilgrims in Medjugorje while the war was going on. There were only about fifty from the United States, being led by a Sister of St. Joseph, and those in our small group of seven. In 1989 the streets were crowded with pilgrims coming back and forth from St. James' Church or from one of the apparition sites. Now the streets were practically empty. During the night we heard bombing in the distance, but our Blessed Mother was still appearing every day to the visionaries. I noticed a strong heavenly aroma at the time of her appearance to the visionaries in the church. What a wonderful experience, and how grateful I was!

One of the days during our visit, we climbed what is called "Apparition Hill." This is the spot where our Blessed Mother appeared on the second day of her visitation in 1981. The Sisters of St. Joseph and her group had arrived there before us and were praying. There was a Cross marking the place where Our Lady had been seen by the children, and flowers were placed there by the people in gratitude and petition. I noticed a young man who had separated himself a short distance from his group to pray at this special site in front of the Cross. His body was trembling as he quietly shed many tears. When he got up to join his group I decided to go and pray at the same spot he had just left. All of the sudden, I felt someone I couldn't see, loving me. Never have I felt such love, it filled my whole being and I began to cry my eyes out. I felt like a changed person, and as I descended Apparition Hill I felt full of love for everyone. What a gift from Our Lady! Eventually, as time passed, I was back to my old self with many faults to work on!

There was a man from Canada who came to Medjugorje at the same time we were there. Upon hearing that our priest chaplain was Canadian he visited us, and eventually he spoke privately to Father in another room. How happy he was when he came out! He told our group he had scheduled two other times to go to Medjugorje, and both times he had to cancel from making the pilgrimage because of one problem or another. After meeting and talking to Fr. Breault he was so grateful to God and our Blessed Mother that his other trips did not materialize and was drawn to come to this oasis of peace when he did. His face revealed a soul filled with joy and peace!!

This priest was so special and filled with joy himself that friends of ours, who had met him when he came to the New York area to visit, willingly traveled to Canada to go on a retreat he was giving on two separate occasions. My mother-in-law Betty and her friend Sophie, also the mothers of two of our friends were invited and came, and were very grateful they joined us. One of the mothers started going to daily Mass after she got back home!

Father told us a wonderful story! There was a certain man from Canada who was planning a trip to Medjugorje. He had a notebook into which he invited family and friends to write their petitions to our Blessed Mother. He promised to bring their requests with him on pilgrimage to present them to Our Lady during one of her apparitions. He even asked his Bishop if he would like to sign his book. The Bishop said, "Yes, I will sign it," and he also asked our Blessed Mother to bless his whole diocese.

Well, when this particular man climbed what they call, "Cross Mountain" on the evening when our Blessed Mother had told one of the visionaries that she would be present for an apparition while they prayed on the mountain, he held up his notebook and asked our Blessed Mother to bless everyone who signed it. He then heard within himself, "Yes, I will bless them, and

I will also bless them at my mother's house, my spouse's house, and my house." "Blessed Mother, I don't know what you mean", he answered in response. Then within himself he heard, "You will know when you go down the mountain." As he was climbing down the mountain he realized, "My mother's house", St. Anne de Beaupre, in Quebec, "My spouse's house", St. Joseph's Oratory, in Montréal, "My house", Cap de la Madeleine, in Tres Rivoire. No wonder we feel blessed when we go to these special shrines!

Later on I thought of the times my husband and I have visited the National Shrine of the Immaculate Conception in Washington, D.C., on the way to our time share in Florida, and what a blessing it has always been to go to Mass there, pray the Rosary in the chapel dedicated to Our Lady of Lourdes, take advantage of the opportunity of going to Confession, and visit all the other wonderful shrines there. Especially beautiful is the Chapel where the Blessed Sacrament is reposed. Come and see!

On July 11, 1985 Our Lady's message was: "Dear children! Today I am begging you to put more blessed objects in your homes, and that every person should carry blessed objects on himself. Let everything be blessed so that Satan will tempt you less because you are armed against him. Thank you for your response to my call."

The most important message, Our Lady said, is conversion. She is asking us to pray from our hearts. "Let Holy Mass be your life." Pray the Rosary, do penance, read the Bible, fast, go to confession monthly, accept Divine Peace and spread it.

More can be learned about the apparitions at Medjugorje, and the monthly messages of Our Lady Queen of Peace to the world at www.medjugorje.hr where you can read all the messages of Our Lady from 1984 to the present time. Another website that also includes live coverage is: www.marytv.tv

St. James Church in Medjugorje

Shrine to Our Lady in St. James Church

Apparition Hill, Medjugorje

One of the visionaries, Vicka, giving a talk
through her interpreter

Included in our latest trip to Medjugorje was a visit to Wadowice, Poland, the birthplace of the late Pope John Paul II. We were brought to the three-room apartment where he, the young Karol Wojtyla, lived for a number of years as he was growing up. Imagine our reaction when our guide pointed out the view from his bedroom window. Across the narrow street is the church where he was baptized and was a parishioner. On the outside wall, clearly visible, was a large clock which had the inscription in Polish, "Time is running, eternity is waiting." Can you imagine seeing that message every day outside your window growing up? It must have had quite an effect on young Karol.

We also visited the horror of the concentration camp in Auschwitz where untold numbers of Jews, Poles and others were murdered and burned to ashes in the ovens. Behind one glass wall there were a couple of tons of human hair taken from the prisoners, and behind another, dolls and toys. How heartbreaking it was to witness the cruelty of men toward their fellow humans.

In another section of the camp we saw the prison cell where Fr. Maximilian Kolbe, a Franciscan priest, O.F.M. Conv., was sentenced to death by starvation. He offered his life in exchange for the life of another prisoner, who had cried out in anguish about his wife and children. This prisoner was picked to die along with nine others as a punishment because three other prisoners had escaped. Maximilian, the only survivor of the ten who were without food and water for two weeks, was given a lethal injection because the guards wanted his bunker for another prisoner. The man for whom Maximilian gave his life, Franciszek Gajowniczek, survived the war and later, in his 90s, was able to be present at Maximilian's canonization in Rome, as a saint of the Church on October 10, 1982.

When we opened the gate to leave the prison camp it greatly saddened me that the poor souls who had been imprisoned there were not as free to leave as we were. Visiting Auschwitz was a heart-rending experience.

To learn more about St. Maximilian contact the National Shrine of St. Maximilian Kolbe, Marytown, at: 1600 W. Park Av., Libertyville, IL. 60048, 1-847-367-7800, www.marytown.com

~~~~~~~~~~

We visited the city of Krakow where Karol Wojtyla (the future Pope John Paul II) studied for the priesthood, although secretly until after the war, because of the presence of the Nazis in Poland during World War II. In 1967 he was named Cardinal of Krakow by Pope Paul VI.

In Krakow is the Basilica of Divine Mercy, the construction of which was begun in the 1990s, and then upon completion was consecrated by Pope John Paul II on August 17, 2002. A great number of people from all over the world visit this special site. A painting of Jesus, The Divine Mercy, His right hand raised in blessing, with red and pale rays emanating from His garment slightly drawn aside at the breast and with the inscription beneath it, "Jesus, I Trust in You" (in Polish) is in the main church beyond and above the altar. Our Lord had asked Sister Faustina Kowalska to have a painting made of this Image, with the inscription, that He revealed to her in a vision.

When the first painting was done, according to her description, Faustina was so disappointed she went to the chapel and cried because the beauty of Our Lord wasn't shown as she knew it. She said to Jesus, "Who will paint You as beautiful as You are?" Then she heard the words:

"Not in the beauty of the color nor of the brush lies the greatness of this image, but in My grace." (*Diary,* 313).

"I am offering people a vessel with which they are to keep coming for graces to the fountain of mercy. That vessel is this image with the

signature: *"Jesus, I trust in You."* (*Diary,* 327)

"By means of this image I shall grant many graces to souls. It is to be a reminder of the demands of My mercy, because even the strongest faith is of no avail without works." (*Diary,* 742).

A number of renditions of the Image have been painted since Sr. Faustina directed the painting of the first one in 1934.

Our Lord Jesus entrusted to Sr. Faustina, a member of the Congregation of the Sisters of Mercy, through numerous visions and revelations, His Message of Mercy which He wanted her to have proclaimed throughout the world. He said,

"Mankind will not have peace until it turns with trust to My mercy." (Diary, 300).

"...before I come as a just Judge, I first open wide the door of My mercy. He who refuses to pass through the door of My mercy must pass through the door of My justice..." (Diary, 1146).

I especially loved visiting the Sisters'

Chapel which is open to the public. Sister Faustina lived on this earth only 33 years, having been born on August 25, 1905, and died in the odor of sanctity on October 5, 1938. The casket containing her bodily remains is in this chapel, under one of the earliest paintings of the Image of the Divine Mercy.

Jesus told Sister Faustina,

"I promise that the soul that will venerate this image will not perish. I also promise victory over [its] enemies already here on earth, especially at the hour of death. I Myself will defend it as My own glory." (Diary, 48)

"Oh, if sinners knew My mercy, they would not perish in such great numbers. Tell sinful souls not to be afraid to approach Me; speak to them of My great mercy....The loss of each soul plunges Me into mortal sadness. You always console Me when you pray for sinners. The prayer most pleasing to Me is prayer for the conversion of sinners. Know, My daughter, that this prayer is always heard and answered." (Diary, 1396-97)

"I never reject a contrite heart." (Diary, 1485)

"The greater the sinner, the greater the right he has to My mercy." (Diary, 723)

"...no soul that has called upon My mercy has been disappointed or brought to shame." (Diary, 1541)

Jesus also spoke to her about the importance of being merciful to others.

"...But write this for the many souls who are often worried because they do not have the material means with which to carry out an act of mercy. Yet spiritual mercy, which requires neither permissions nor storehouses, is much more meritorious and is within the grasp of every soul. If a soul does not exercise mercy somehow or other, it will not obtain My mercy on the day of judgment. ..." (Diary, 1317)

Our Lord revealed to Sr. Faustina that He wanted the first Sunday after Easter to be made known as the Feast of The Divine Mercy. He told her:

"On that day, the very depths of My tender mercy are open. I pour out a whole ocean of graces upon those souls who approach the

fount of My mercy. The soul that will go to Confession and receive Holy Communion shall obtain complete forgiveness of sins and punishment." (Diary, 699).

"To receive the grace of Divine Mercy Sunday, you simply need to go to Confession before or on the day of the feast---sometime during Lent suffices; be in the state of grace (no mortal sin); and receive Holy Communion with the intention of obtaining the promised grace." (MPL2 leaflet: Marian Press, Stockbridge, MA. 01263)

Pope John Paul II, on April 30, 2000, during his homily at the canonization of Sister Faustina declared that the second Sunday of Easter throughout the Church will be called "Divine Mercy Sunday."

A great number of Catholic Churches have the Divine Mercy Image in their Churches for the veneration and benefit of the people. Reproductions of the Image with the inscription, "Jesus, I trust in You," have been promulgated throughout the world.

They are available at the Marians of the

Immaculate Conception, Stockbridge, MA 01263, 1-800-462-7426, ShopMercy.org, or at any Catholic gift store.

N.B. Quotations are from the diary of Saint Faustina.

A SPECIAL VISIT TO THE SHRINE OF THE IMMACULATE CONCEPTION

A number of years ago we decided to stop overnight in Georgetown on our way down south to Florida, and planned to visit the National Shrine of the Immaculate Conception in Washington, D.C. the next day. We had brought with us some cheese and crackers and a bottle of wine to have on the night of our arrival. There was a small table and chairs in the room in which we stayed overnight, and I prepared the table for a little repast. After leaving the bathroom Ed started to prepare the cheese and crackers. Somehow I decided to ask him, "Did you wash your hands?" Well, he became so annoyed with me that he wouldn't speak to me, which is not our usual way of handling our annoyances with each other. We always speak to each other even if we are annoyed, at least after a very short time of silence, but he wouldn't speak to me for the rest of the night or even into the next morning.

It was very quiet in the car on the way to the Shrine. After we parked and got out of the car Ed said to me, "You go your way, I'll go mine." On our previous visits we usually walked down the aisle to the Blessed Sacrament chapel, visiting the different shrines more or less together on the way. This time, he obviously didn't want to do that. He didn't seem to want any part of me.

As you enter the church, in the main vestibule there is a beautiful bronze statue of Our Lady of Fatima on the right side of the entrance doors and a lovely bronze statue of St. Theresa, the Little Flower of Jesus, on the left. I decided to go first to Our Lady and pour out my heart and soul to her. I'm not a crier, but as I prayed I cried quite a few tears. Then I heard within myself, "Our Lord wants to see you," and so I immediately proceeded to the Blessed Sacrament chapel without stopping at any of the shrines on the way down the aisle to where the chapel is located. There I knelt in prayer, before Our Lord and soon I heard within myself, "I know he's difficult to live with, but so are you," and then He said, "It is through your marriage that you will work out your eternal salvation." I knew these words were from Our Lord Jesus because, to be honest, I wouldn't have said to myself, "And so are you." These words from him gave me much peace.

Meanwhile, unbeknown to me, my husband Ed had been praying a little further back in the chapel. He came up to me and said, "Jackie,

I was thinking as I looked at the Cross, if Our Lord could forgive, I can forgive you." In the meantime I was thinking, "He should be asking *me* to forgive him," but I let it go. After the special gifts Our Lord and His Blessed Mother had just given me, how could I not? We gave each other a kiss, and that was the end of our disagreement. After the rest of our visit was over, we left the church walking hand-in-hand down the steps and the sidewalk to where our car was parked. Praise to the Blessed Mother for obtaining such a beautiful grace of healing for us!

When we got home after our visit to Florida, I told my confessor everything that had happened. He confirmed that Our Lord did speak to me, and he said that it was a great grace. Sometime later our friend, Fr. Breault, came to visit us. I also related to him everything that had happened. He told me, "You humiliated him," meaning Ed, and I knew he hit the nail right on the head. That thought never entered my mind. In a flash I understood that I was part of the problem! God bless him!

"When I say, "My foot is slipping,"/ your
kindness, O LORD, sustains me;
When cares abound within me, / your comfort
gladdens my soul."
(Psalm 94:18-19)

We are very blessed to have a very beautiful Adoration Chapel in our parish Church of St. Marguerite Bourgeoys, Brookfield, CT that has Adoration of the Blessed Sacrament from 9:00 a.m. to 5:00 p.m. every day of the year, except when there is ice or snow. Besides his rosary Ed still brings a spiritual book, his favorite being "He and I" by Gabrielle Bossis, a Catholic layperson and mystic who lived in France in the 20th century (1874-1950). A Salesian priest, Fr. August Bosio, S.D.B. whom Ed & I knew from the Marian Shrine in West Haverstraw, N.Y. was a great promoter of "He and I" as it has an Imprimatur by Msgr. Jean-Marie Fortier, Archbishop of Sherbrooke, Quebec, November 14, 1969 and has been translated into many languages. It has been an inspiration to a vast number of people. It is a journal of the dialogue of "the Inner Voice" and Gabrielle which she perceived to be the Voice of Christ.

Those interested in obtaining a copy may do so by contacting:

The Daughters of St. Paul 212-754-1110; www.pauline.org

SAINT ANN, THE MOTHER OF MARY, THE GRANDMOTHER OF JESUS

Recently, when I looked over the mail of the day, I noticed on one of the envelopes the statement that inside there was a relic of Saint Ann from the Blessed Sacrament Fathers and Brothers at St. Ann's Shrine in Cleveland, Ohio. When I opened the letter it contained a beautiful plasticized picture of St. Ann with her young daughter Mary, the Mother of Jesus. In the upper left-hand corner under the plastic there was a piece of cloth that had been touched to St. Ann's relic. A relic is an object, a part of the body, clothes, or article associated with a saint that remains as a memorial of the departed saint. On the back of the card was a beautiful prayer to St. Ann, requesting her intercession. I showed the prayer card to my husband and we both kissed the relic before we prayed our rosary.

On the previous day, I had exhausted myself by trying to accomplish more than I could handle physically at my age. And so the day I received the prayer card with the relic I was wiped out and feeling down on myself. After we prayed our Rosary I decided to pray the prayers on the back of the holy card for all the people that were in my intentions at that time. When I finished the prayers, immediately all my tiredness left me and I was filled with joy! I wasn't even praying for myself. St. Ann helped me without my even asking her!

Then I remembered an experience that had happened many years before. I was very upset about something that was taking place in my life at that time. I noticed in the Catholic New York, which was our diocesan newspaper that a novena to St. Ann in preparation for her feast day, July 26th, was going to be held at St. Jean the Baptiste Catholic church in New York City. In this church there is a shrine to Saint Ann and a small portion of the relic venerated at the Basilica of St. Anne de Beaupré in Quebec, Canada. (In French, Ann is spelled "Anne." "Beaupré" is the name of the town). A piece of that same relic is also venerated at St. Ann's Shrine in Cleveland.

I decided to go down to New York by train and bus to honor St. Ann on her feast day and to ask for her intercession. There were quite a number of people in the church and many were ahead of me praying in front of her statue and relic. Even though I wasn't close, I felt so blessed and filled with joy. I remember smiling at everyone on the bus on the way back home. The disturbance I had been experiencing was removed from me and I was filled with peace. I was so very grateful to St. Ann and Our Lord for easing my mind and comforting me.

After sending a donation to the Blessed Sacrament Fathers, I just *had* to write a separate note to "Fr. M.," the spiritual director of the shrine, to thank him for following the inspiration to send the relic card of St. Ann to us and to all the others who received one. I received a lovely letter in return, thanking me for my note in which I included what happened to me when I prayed the prayers on the card. Fr. M. wrote, "….the relic with which we blessed the prayer card, as well as St. Ann's oil, is a part of the relic at St. Anne de Beaupré and we have received many letters telling of benefits through these."

When Fr. M. mentioned St. Ann's oil in his letter it brought to my mind a special favor from St. Ann that happened a few years ago. One of our daughters was going through a difficult time in her life. I had a bottle of St. Ann's oil that had been sent to me. I gave it to our daughter since she has a devotion to St. Ann. She told me sometime later that she blessed herself every night with the oil and felt very much comforted.

A few days later I called St. Ann's Shrine

to see if I could obtain 25 more of these prayer cards. I told the woman who answered the phone what had happened to me, and she was elated with my story. I was so happy to hear her say I could send for additional prayer cards. "Just send us a letter and ask for the relic card," she said. I asked her what the usual donation was. When she told me the offering I was surprised at how little was required. What a great gift for such a small donation!

Soon the relic cards arrived in the mail. The very next day the sister of the president of our local Legion of Mary* at St. Joseph's Church in Brookfield, CT. was having heart surgery. I hurriedly brought over two of the relic prayer cards to St. Ann for my president to pick up at the church, one for her and one for her sister. She brought the prayer card to her sister the next day when she went to see her in the hospital. She prayed earnestly to St. Ann, in addition to her other prayers, for a successful operation for her sister. The operation went very well. Although her sister was in intensive care for several days, when she left the hospital she was able to go directly home. She had tolerable pain and was able to resume her normal activities such as driving, etc. much before the time expected. Both sisters were and are extremely grateful for the intercession and help of Saint Ann.

*The Legion of Mary is a worldwide apostolic organization of Catholic men and women, who with the guidance of the church, and under the banner of Mary, and with her help, seek to bring the love and mercy of Our Lord Jesus Christ to those they meet in the varied works of the Legion, including the visitation of the sick and the elderly.

Our Catholic youth are also encouraged to join the Legion to participate in the apostolic works appropriate for their age. In the village of Kibeho, which is located in Rwanda, Africa, (an apparition site of our Blessed Mother already approved by the Church), Our Lady asked one of the visionaries, Alphonsine, to join the Legion of Mary and she readily agreed. One of the other visionaries, Anathalie, a seventeen-year-old student had been a member of the Legion and other Catholic youth groups for many years.

"The Legion of Mary presents the true face of the Catholic Church." (Pope John XXIII)

In the year of 2005, our local parish of St. Marguerite Bourgeoys, sponsored a pilgrimage by bus, led by Fr. Peter Towsley our parish priest. The trip included visiting some of the major shrines of Canada: the Basilicas of St. Joseph's Oratory and Notre Dame in Montreal, and the Basilica of Sainte Anne de Beaupré, thirty miles east of Quebec City (St. Anne's major shrine in North America). On our way to St. Anne's, we visited the Canadian National Shrine to our Blessed Mother, the Basilica of Cap-de-la-Madeleine (Our Lady of the Cape) in Trois Rivieres. Don't miss visiting the very beautiful original chapel if you go!

Of course, our pilgrimage included going to the Chapel of Notre-Dame-de-Bon-Secours (Our Lady of Good Help) in Old Montreal where the remains of our parish patron, Saint Marguerite, lie in repose in the sanctuary, having been transferred to that church only a week or two before we began our journey. St. Marguerite, a Canadian saint, founded the Sisters of the Congregation of Notre Dame, and is also considered to be the co-foundress of Montreal. Next to the chapel there is a museum about her life and the early history of Montreal.

Prayer to St. Marguerite Bourgeoys:

O Saint Marguerite Bourgeoys, grant that like you I may place all my trust in Jesus my Saviour, and in Our Lady of Good Help, in order that, through your intercession, I may obtain the grace which I so ardently desire.

Say 3 times: Glory be to the Father and to the Son and to the Holy Spirit as it was in the beginning, is now and ever shall be, world without end. Amen.

Reprinted with the permission of the Ordinary, Montreal, Oct. 31, 1982.

And what a beautiful pilgrimage it was! At Sainte Anne's Basilica in Canada there are quite a number of crutches that were left there at the shrine by people who had been healed of their infirmities because of their faith in her intercession.

I remember many years ago our friend Fr. Breault spoke to us about his brother Alphonse, who was confined to a wheelchair for quite some time. When he was twelve years old, their mother brought him to St. Anne's Shrine in Canada. As she wheeled her son up to the church, Alphonse prayed interiorly, "St. Anne, if you heal me, I will become a priest." All of a sudden he got out of his wheelchair and walked, and this happened before they even entered the church! Eventually he made good his promise. Rev. Alphonse Breault, O.M.I. was ordained a priest in 1925 and entered eternal life October 3, 1970, having been a priest for 45 years. How powerful are the prayers of the mother of the Blessed Virgin Mary, and the grandmother of Jesus, St. Ann!

Prayer to St. Ann

Glorious St. Ann, filled with compassion for those who invoke you and with love for those who suffer, I humbly ask you to take my following request under your special protection (mention your request). Please recommend it to your daughter Mary and present it before the throne of Jesus so that He may grant my request. Above all, obtain for me the grace of one day seeing my God face to face and with you, Mary and all the saints, praising and blessing Him for all eternity. Amen.

Good St. Ann, Mother of Mary who is our life, our sweetness and our hope, pray to her for me and obtain my request. (Say 3 times).

St. Anne de Beaupré

Our Lady of the Cape

St. Joseph's Oratory

THE "FLYING" NOVENA

A number of years ago, my husband and I went on a retreat for married couples. The priest who gave the weekend, Fr. Andrew Apostoli, C.F.R., shared with us a wonderful story about Mother Teresa. Mother Teresa and her Sisters, when they needed something in a hurry, would pray what Mother called the "Flying" Novena. It consisted of praying nine Memorares in a row.

When Mother Teresa's Order, The Missionaries of Charity, had a convent behind the Iron Curtain, the superior of the convent became seriously ill and had to go back to India for treatment. None of the other sisters at their convent were capable at that time to take her place. Mother Teresa telephoned the appropriate government office in charge of giving out visas. When Mother explained her problem, the officer in charge told her she had to wait six months before she could obtain a visa for the sister she wanted to send to replace the ailing nun. Mother Teresa politely accepted his answer, but after the phone call she and her sisters began to pray nine Memorares in a row to our Blessed Mother to help them obtain a visa without delay from the Communist government. She needed to send one of her sisters from India, whom she knew would be able to take over the other sister's position as superior. After the sisters completed the nine prayers, the telephone rang, and the officer Mother Teresa had previously spoken to told her, once again, that he could not obtain a visa for her for several months.

Mother Teresa remained agreeable with him, but after hanging up, she again asked her sisters to pray with her another nine Memorares. At the eighth Memorare the telephone rang again! Lo and behold, it was the same officer. "Mother, you can have the visa you requested immediately," he said. Mother Teresa and her sisters were so very grateful to our Blessed Mother for answering their prayers so quickly.

Since hearing this story, I have prayed this very efficacious novena when I've needed something important in a hurry, with wonderful results!

The Memorare

Remember, O most gracious Virgin Mary, that never was it known, that anyone who fled to your protection, implored your help, or sought your intercession was left unaided.

Inspired with this confidence, I fly unto you, O Virgin of virgins, my Mother. To you do I come, before you I stand, sinful and sorrowful. O Mother of the Word Incarnate, despise not my petitions, but in your mercy hear and answer me. Amen.

~~~~~~~~~~

My husband and I had signed up for a Marian Shrine Pilgrimage, which was something that he wanted to give me as a delayed 60th birthday gift. We were not originally scheduled to go on the particular tour we eventually went with, as we had signed up with a different company for a similar tour, going to all the places that we wanted to visit, and had paid the $5,000 or so fee. But then we got a notice about a month before the trip, that they had changed their itinerary which included a place we had no desire to go to, and canceled a visit to one of the shrines we really wanted to see!

At first we were in a quandary as to what to do about it, but then we decided to look into other tour company's pilgrimages. How thankful we were to find another tour that we were very happy with, scheduled to leave a week or so later, that would bring us to Fatima in time for the anniversary of the miracle of the sun, on October 13th. Of course we had to pay another $5,000 plus and that left us short of more than $10,000, unless and until, we got our first $5,000 back. Well, let me tell you it was not that easy!

We called our travel agent, and we called the tour company to cancel the first trip, because it wasn't what we wanted, or what we had signed up for. The tour company said, after a number of requests, that a check was in the mail, but it never came. My husband was getting very upset, and so I decided to pray the "Flying Novena." "Blessed Mother" I prayed, "Eddie is getting very upset," and then I asked her to please help us out with this situation. Ordinarily I don't like to pray about material things, but I could see that Ed's annoyance was not a good thing.

Another call was made to the tour company, and within a few days a total return of our money for the canceled trip was sent to us. We were so grateful to our Blessed Mother for hearing and answering our prayers. Also, this newly planned tour was the one that was leaving New York City the day *after* Pope John Paul II's Mass in Central Park, in October of 1995. What a blessing it was to be present at our saintly

Pope's Mass! Thanks be to Our Lady and Divine
Providence!

POPE JOHN PAUL II'S VISIT
TO CENTRAL PARK

A couple of weeks before we were to leave on our pilgrimage my back started to bother me. Our itinerary included visits to Fatima in Portugal; the Miraculous Medal Shrine in Paris; Lourdes in southern France, and Medjugorje in Bosnia, Herzegovina (in the former Yugoslavia). This was our second visit to Lourdes, but Ed's first to Medjugorje, and the first visit for both of us to Fatima and Paris. The closer we got to our departure date the worse my back was getting. When my back goes out, I can't even carry a handbag! And here we were going on a two-week trip the day after Pope John Paul II was offering the Holy Sacrifice of the Mass in Central Park in New York City.

We had received tickets from our parish to be present at the Holy Father's Mass. I was really concerned about whether or not we should take advantage of our tickets, or would it be wiser to give them to someone else. I made a decision to, "Step out in faith" and go to the Pope's Mass.

There was a chartered bus in our area for those going down to Central Park for the occasion. We couldn't get over how many buses were parked on Fifth Avenue and how long of a walk it was to get to where we had to go! (Long walks, when my back is acting up, usually makes things worse). We finally got to the area that our tickets designated. We knew ahead of time that we had to bring our own chairs since we wouldn't be that close to the main altar. There was a large video screen and sound system set up in our area and other areas around the park, so that the tremendous crowd of people could participate in the Mass more fully. It was a beautiful liturgy, and I was so glad we came without even knowing what was going to happen!

When Pope John Paul II gave his final blessing at the end of the Mass, "May almighty God bless you, the Father, and the Son, and the Holy Spirit," all of a sudden I felt a movement inside my back and all my pain disappeared! My back felt fine throughout our whole two-week trip, which started the next day!! Praise God!! Anyone can imagine how grateful I felt because I didn't even pray to be healed, I just decided to, "Step out in faith" and go to Pope John Paul II's Mass in Central Park, no matter what!!

A MARIAN SHRINE PILGRIMAGE

We departed as I just mentioned, the day after Pope John Paul II's special Mass in Central Park, New York, full of gratitude that my back felt fine and we were able to go on this blessed pilgrimage.

A trip to Lourdes was always special for us. Before we left, one of our friends, who makes rosaries out of wood branches obtained from pilgrimage sites, asked me to bring back a small branch of wood from each of the holy places we visited so she could whittle wooden beads from them. When we were in Lourdes I didn't notice any fallen branches, but lo and behold, as Ed and I started to walk up the path to the Stations of the Cross, off to the side I saw one branch of wood. Everywhere else the grass was completely manicured. How ecstatic I was! I knew this was a special gift from heaven. I gratefully picked it up and carried it with us while we prayed at each Station; my first branch.

How blessed it always is to pray at Lourdes with people from all over the world, and to honor Our Lady with them during a candlelight procession at night!

We were in Fatima for the anniversary of

Our Lady's final apparition there which took place on October 13, 1917. That was the day the "Miracle of the Sun" took place in answer to Our Lady's promise of a miracle so that the people would believe in her message given through the children, Lucia, Francisco and Jacinta. According to the newspapers there were approximately 500,000 people in Fatima while we were there on October 13, 1995. So many people walked there on pilgrimage to honor Our Lady on that special anniversary day.

How wonderful it was to be there, with all those other faithful people, praying reverently in the open square in front of the Church. There is a beautiful outdoor chapel that was built very close to the tree where Our Lady first appeared on a cloud to the children. The absolute perfection of the tree and its leaves was marvelous to behold! One couldn't help but be taken aback in admiration of it.

At one point, a statue of Our Lady of Fatima was carried through the crowd on a bier that was covered with flowers, while the people sang a hymn to our Blessed Mother. Then the statue was placed near the altar and the Holy Sacrifice of the Mass soon began. After Mass Our Lady's statue was carried away while all sang and waved their handkerchiefs, as is the custom there, in a loving goodbye.

The first apparition to the three children began on May 13, 1917, and continued on the thirteenth of each of the following months until October 13 when the miracle promised by Our Lady took place.

Sometime in the 1960's I was at the kitchen sink doing dishes, when my attention was drawn to the interview being broadcast on the radio which I had on while I was working. A gentleman who had been present in Fatima at the time of the "miracle of the sun" in 1917 described what he saw! He said it was raining very heavily and the people who were there, about fifty to seventy thousand in number, were absolutely soaked, but this did not deter them from waiting to see if anything was going to happen. Some of the skeptics started to complain and make fun of the children as they waited for what the skeptics thought was something that was not going to take place.

After Our Lady spoke to Lucia she raised her hand to the sun that had come out and started spinning in the sky, flashing beautiful colors. All of a sudden the sun started coming toward the earth and the people began screaming, "It's the end of the world!" Some cried aloud to God begging forgiveness for their sins, the skeptics were converted, and many were healed of their illnesses. Soon the sun went back up into the sky, and the people began noticing that their clothes which were soaking wet were now completely dry! And not only that, their garments that were stained by the mud were now clean! The ground that was so muddy was also dry! The miracle that was promised, happened! Praise God! How grateful I was to have heard, very unexpectedly, this man's eye witness account over the radio that day!

In all six of her apparitions Our Lady asked for prayer, penance, and sacrifices, and especially the daily recitation of the Rosary. After each decade of the Rosary Our Lady requested that we pray the following prayer: "O my Jesus, forgive us our sins, save us from the fires of hell, lead all souls to Heaven, especially those in most need of Thy mercy." She said that God wishes to establish in the world devotion to her Immaculate Heart. She asked that the, "Five First Saturday Devotion" be established in the Church.

The Five First Saturdays in Reparation to the
Immaculate Heart of Mary

Our Blessed Mother promised that everyone who, on the first Saturday of five consecutive months, shall go to confession, receive Holy Communion, recite five decades of the Rosary, and keep her company for fifteen minutes while meditating on the fifteen mysteries of the Rosary, with the intention of making reparation to her, she promised to assist them, at the hour of death, with all the graces needed for the salvation of their souls.

Our Lady told Jacinta, "The sins which cause most souls to go to hell are the sins of the flesh." She also said that, "Fashions will much offend Our Lord. People who serve God should not follow the fashions." And with a sad expression, Our Lady asked that we, "Pray, pray very much, and make sacrifices for sinners; for many souls go to hell, because there are none to sacrifice themselves and to pray for them." Looking very sad, Our Lady said: "Do not offend the Lord our God anymore, because He is already so much offended." The children made many sacrifices for the conversion of sinners. Jacinta said, **"If people knew what eternity is,**

they would convert."

Our Lady also prophesied that Russia would spread her errors, (atheistic communism) throughout the world, and that in the end Russia would be converted, her Immaculate Heart would triumph, and there would be an era of peace.

Jacinta and Francisco died very young. Lucia eventually became a Dorothean Sister in Túy, Spain in 1925. After many years as a Dorothean Sister she requested and was granted permission to become a Carmelite and was transferred to the Carmel of Saint Teresa in Coimbra, Portugal in 1948. She stressed the importance of the offering up of the sacrifices entailed in the accomplishment of our daily duties. She said that the Rosary and the Brown Scapular of Our Lady of Mount Carmel were the prime means to help us to be faithful to the demands of daily duty. Our Lord himself told Sr. Lucia that the penance He now required is the sacrifice necessary to keep his laws and to fulfill the duties required by our state in life.

While we were in Fatima we had a tour guide who took us to all the special places. One was a lovely secluded spot where the Angel of Portugal appeared to the three children, Lucia,

Francesco, and Jacinta. Our guide described the vision to us.

A Sacred Host was suspended in the air above the hands of the angel. The three children knelt down in adoration while the angel taught them these prayers:

"My God! I believe, I adore, I hope and I love You! I ask You pardon for all those who do not believe, do not adore, do not hope and do not love You." He taught them to repeat these words three times.

The other prayer the angel taught the children is as follows---

"Most Holy Trinity, Father, Son, and Holy Spirit, I adore You profoundly, and I offer You the most precious Body, Blood, Soul and Divinity of Jesus Christ, present in all the tabernacles of the world, in reparation for the outrages, sacrileges, and indifference with which He Himself is offended. And through the infinite merits of His most Sacred Heart and the Immaculate Heart of Mary, I beg of you the conversion of poor sinners."

There were in this area beautiful statues

of the angel and the three children commemorating this event. It was on a small hill and a number of people were visiting the spot at the same time. After we prayed at the apparition site most of the people started to leave the area and only a few remained.

I decided that this was a good place to look for a branch for our friend who makes the rosaries. I picked up a branch that had fallen to the ground. There were a number of small branches to choose from. All of a sudden, one of the women in the area asked me what I was doing. I told her I was looking for a branch for my friend who makes rosaries out of twigs from branches. She asked me what my friend's name was. I mentioned her name, let's call her Terry, and can you believe it, she told me she knew her! This woman was not in our group but she was present at this special place the same time we were! She told me, "That's not the type of branch Terry uses." She then pointed out the kind of branch that Terry finds most suitable for her rosaries. How happy I was for her help. I went joyfully down the hill of the apparition of the angel gratefully holding, my second branch.

Some of us pilgrims took a side trip to the Carmelite convent in Coimbra, Portugal where

Sister Lucia, the oldest of the visionaries, who was still alive at the time, resided. The Sister who welcomed our group, while we were visiting in the chapel of the convent, told us that if we would like to write our prayer intentions, she would give them to Sister Lucia who would in turn remember them in her prayers. How happy I was to hear this good news! I wrote and I wrote and gratefully gave the sister my prayer petitions when I was finished.

As a cooperator of Opus Dei, and having benefited by a number of Retreats and Days of Recollection given by the priests and members of Opus Dei, I was very surprised and pleased to read in the book, "The Shepherds of Fatima" by M. Fernando Silva: "While she was still in Túy an interesting event occurred. Sister Lucia met (Father) Josemariá Escrivá, founder of Opus Dei.

The Bishop of Túy-Vigo, José López Ortiz arranged this meeting. He had been a friend of Escrivá since their university days in Madrid. The Bishop asked Sister Lucia's superior to allow her to go to the bishop's residence. Sister Lucia and Josemariá Escrivá had never met. All the same, Lucia said emphatically to him: 'Go as soon as possible to Portugal and found Opus Dei there!' He answered that he did not have a passport for Portugal, so she herself offered to negotiate with the civil authorities in the district of Viana do Castelo to facilitate his entry into Portugal. That was in 1945."'*

* The above quote was taken from, "The Shepherds of Fatima" with permission from Pauline Books & Media, who reserve the right that to state that no part of that book may be reproduced in any form or means without written permission from the publisher.

For additional information on the Fatima Message: "Fatima for Today The Urgent Marian Message of Hope" by Fr. Andrew Apostoli, C.F.R., (Ignatius Press, San Francisco, www.ignatius.com)

Note: Fr. Josemariá Escrivá, who founded Opus Dei in 1928 with the purpose of helping people to find holiness in the living out of their daily life, was declared a saint by Pope John Paul II on October 6, 2002. For more information about Opus Dei visit www.opusdei.org

The Basilica of Our Lady of the Rosary of Fatima

Site of the Apparition of the Angel of Peace to
Lucia, Jacinta, and Francisco

Last Vision of Fatima (Trinity Picture) witnessed by
Sister Lucia – June 13, 1929

Note: Permission to include the Trinity Picture -
The Last Vision of Fatima was given by the
World Apostolate of Fatima, Washington, N.J.,
07882

A BRAND NEW ROSARY MAKER

Ed's sister Lorraine is very talented at making crafts. For our 50th wedding anniversary she made us the most beautiful needlepoint of Saint Paul's first letter to the Corinthians 13:4-8, "Love is patient, love is kind..." The scripture was surrounded by lovely flowers and a heart was engraved above all the rest in delicate cross stitch. She said it took her a year to finish. I think she knew we needed a daily reminder of Saint Paul's discourse.

The last time Lorraine came to visit us from her home in the Midwest, I asked her if she would be interested in making rosaries for us. She said she would make them if someone would teach her how. One of the members of our parish, named Natalie, has been making rosaries for years. I called her up and asked her if she would teach Lorraine. She was very happy to have us come to her home to show us how to make them.

Lorraine and I arranged to go to see Natalie to learn her expertise on making rosaries. She was extremely patient with us and gave us some supplies of plastic beads, crosses, centerpieces, and cord so that we could get started. Some of the cord was already cut to the length that Natalie uses. We did fairly well with the first rosary we made at Natalie's house. Lorraine's, I had to admit, turned out much better looking than mine, but Natalie kept on encouraging us.

The Rosary Apostolate is truly a wonderful one. Many people make rosaries for the missions. Others make them for their local parish churches, or for the Catholic patients in a hospital or nursing home. Natalie told us it only takes her about 25 minutes to complete a rosary.

When Lorraine got back home she started to make a rosary with the pre-cut cord. When she tried to attach the cross she found she did not have enough to finish the rosary. She took it apart, and beginning again, cut a longer piece of cord, placing the beads on it as she was shown. When the rosary was completed she was filled with wonder as she suddenly noticed a lovely sweet smell in the room. She told me, "Jackie, I know that scent." She remembered having that same experience as she opened the envelope containing a medal blessed at Medjugorje that I had sent her.

However, she went over to the plastic bag that contained the beads she was using, just to make sure that they did not have the same aroma. They didn't. When she called to tell me all that had happened, we both felt sure that it was our Blessed Mother's presence showing Lorraine her approval and blessing her decision to make rosaries.

We are now blessed with five new rosary makers in our parish! The supplies, which are extremely reasonably priced, are ordered from Our Lady's Rosary Makers in Kentucky. Upon request they will send instructions on how to make a rosary and/or a catalog on supplies available. Anyone interested in learning how to make rosaries can call, write or email:

Our Lady's Rosary Makers
4611 Poplar Level Rd.
Louisville, KY 40213
502-968-1434
mikeford@olrm.org

ST. MICHAEL THE ARCHANGEL

How powerful are the prayers to St. Michael the Archangel! I know this by my own experience. A number of times in the past when Ed and I have had an argument and I realized I was getting too upset, I've gone to our bedroom and prayed the St. Michael prayer repeatedly for a number of times. Soon I would hear the door open and Ed leaning inside saying with the most heartfelt apology, "I'm sorry," with a loving and apologetic smile on his face. How could I stay upset after that? We would forgive each other and once again I'd be very grateful to St. Michael.

The St. Michael Prayer

St. Michael the Archangel, defend us in battle. Be our protection against the wickedness and snares of the devil. May God rebuke him, we humbly pray; and do thou, O Prince of the heavenly host, by the power of God, cast into hell Satan and all the evil spirits who prowl about the world seeking the ruin of souls. Amen.

This prayer was composed by Pope Leo

XIII in 1884 after seeing a vision of Satan and other evil spirits trying to destroy the Church. Even though he saw in the vision St. Michael casting the devils back into hell, he was moved to write this prayer to help defend our faith in this great spiritual warfare. Pope John Paul II urged the faithful to recite this prayer.

A SPECIAL MASS FOR ED'S MOTHER

When Ed's mother was in her seventies, she was diagnosed with the beginnings of Alzheimer's disease. Eventually we realized she needed someone to monitor her medications, and so we arranged to have live-in help for her to do the cooking, cleaning and whatever else was needed to be done in the taking care of Mom. One of our requisites was that the caretaker would bring Mom to Mass on Sundays, which was readily agreed upon by the woman we hired, even though she wasn't Catholic. She was very conscientious about accompanying Mom every Sunday. God bless her! We gave her two days off a week and on those days another woman whom she recommended came to take over.

We often went to visit Mom, most of the time to bring her back to our home for the day, for a family gathering, an overnight, or a two or three day visit which also gave the caregivers a break.

One weekday I drove down to visit Mom early in the day and went to the 9:00 a.m. Mass in her church. I decided to go back to the sacristy when the Mass was over to ask the priest to visit Mom to hear her confession and give her Holy

Communion. He readily agreed. I gave him her address and when I went to Mom's apartment I told her and her caretaker that the priest would be coming to visit. Mom shook her head in agreement and Father came to bring her the sacraments within the next couple of days.

About two years passed by and Mom became much more forgetful. Ed's sister Lorraine, who lived in Illinois, decided to have Mom live with her. Lorraine was still working full-time so she had a woman come in to stay with Mom while she was at work. Eventually a daughter-in-law, Terry, became Mom's caretaker. She would bring Mom to her home during the day, and in nice weather Mom was able to enjoy sitting outdoors. We were very happy about this.

Around seven months before Mom passed away it was deemed necessary, since Mom was waking up during the night and walking around like it was daytime, to have her taken care of in a nursing home. After visiting the nursing homes in the area, Lorraine chose the one she thought best for Mom. When we went out to see the home we readily agreed. It was also located near Mom's granddaughter, Chris, who often went to see her as well.

When Ed's mother passed away on June 14, 1997, her body was flown back to New York to be buried in Calvary cemetery next to her husband Frank. Our family arranged to have her funeral Mass held at Assumption Church in Tuckahoe, New York. It was a beautiful Mass with family and friends present. After the funeral, everyone returned to their respective homes - Ed's sister and her family to the Midwest, and Ed and I back to our summer place in the Catskills.

I called our pastor, Fr. Robert J. McCabe, at St. Thomas Aquinas Church in Forestburgh, New York, to ask him to schedule another Mass for Ed's mother on a Sunday as soon as there was an opening. Because it's a small parish, we were able to arrange to have a Mass rather quickly. When we arrived at church, imagine our surprise when out walked a Bishop and another priest from India, along with our pastor to celebrate the Mass for Ed's mother! The bishop was there to ask for financial assistance for his diocese in India. He introduced his fellow priest, Fr. John Bosco. The Salesian Order was founded by St. John Bosco. In her lifetime, Ed's mother was a promoter for the Salesians!

Before going to live with Lorraine, Mom

belonged to a neighborhood club in the Bronx. She always kept a supply of Mass cards on hand from the Salesians for her friends. When a relative or friend of a club member became ill or passed away, Mom was often asked for one of the cards. She or they would then send the name of the deceased or sick person, with a donation to the Salesians, so that their loved one would be remembered in the Salesians' Masses, prayers, and good works.

Mom and her sister Elsie would travel to West Haverstraw, New York to visit the Marian Shrine and Retreat Center of Mary Help of Christians, which is staffed by the Salesians, for a special day of Confession, Mass and Communion at their beautiful Chapel and grounds of 200 acres. This was a day of pilgrimage for them for a number of summers. Lorraine also visited the Shrine with Mom. She told me how much she loved it there, and how beautiful she thought it was!

How happy it made us to see a Bishop and a priest named Fr. John Bosco offer a Mass, together with our pastor, for Ed's mom!

"Give thanks to the LORD, for he is good, for his mercy endures forever." (Psalm 118:1)

THE HOLY SHROUD OF TURIN

The year of 1998 was a memorable year for my husband Ed and me. We would be celebrating our 45th wedding anniversary in November, and we decided to go on a pilgrimage in April of the same year to see the Holy Shroud of Our Lord in Turin, Italy which was going to be shown for the first time in twenty years. The Shroud is, according to the belief of many Christians, the burial cloth of Our Lord and Savior, Jesus Christ. Our pilgrimage would also include visits to Rome, Assisi, Siena, Pisa, and La Salette.

The trip began with the privilege of attending Pope John Paul II's Mass on Holy Thursday. In fact, we were supposed to arrive from New York on Holy Thursday afternoon with plenty of time to check into our hotel and rest a while before heading over to the Basilica of St. John Lateran in Rome where the Pope would be celebrating the Mass. We traveled all night by plane and arrived on schedule in Europe, only to be told that our connecting flight to Rome was going to be delayed by a couple of hours. When we finally arrived at our hotel, we were told to hurry and come right down to the lobby after we checked into our room so we could get back on the bus and be transported to the Basilica. How I longed to lie down for at least twenty minutes since I wasn't able to sleep on the plane. But no, there was no time for that, and of course we didn't want to miss the Pope's Mass, especially on Holy Thursday.

Our tour guide had tickets for reserved seats so at least we would be able to sit until the Mass began, or so we thought! When we arrived at the Basilica we were led down the aisle and we could see there were quite a number of reserved seats. Our group was very pleased to see them, but can you imagine how we felt when the usher would not allow us to sit down even though we had tickets?! So we were the first ones standing behind the empty seats and we arrived two hours before the Mass was scheduled to begin! I was so tired from being on the plane all night long. After standing for some time, I started to think, "I can't do this, I just can't do this. I'm so exhausted!" My legs were really starting to give out. I seriously thought about leaving and taking a taxi back to the hotel to lie down and rest. But I immediately thought, "How can I possibly miss Mass on Holy Thursday with the Pope celebrating!" I've been going to Mass on Holy

Thursday since grammar school, and this year to have Mass with the Pope was extra special! "I just can't do this!" I thought again, but I just couldn't give in to my tiredness.

More people started to enter the Cathedral and it started to get very crowded with standing room only, except for the reserved seats. A woman pushed herself ahead of me. Where we were standing we were first in line, and our view of the altar was unobstructed. When I showed her my annoyance, she just looked at me and stayed where she was! I was not happy about her unwillingness to move back.

After a while I started to pray the Rosary. When I came to the third Joyful Mystery, the Birth of Our Lord, I prayed for peace in the world. As I was praying I realized, "I'm praying for peace in the world and I'm not at peace with this woman!" I decided to tap her on the shoulder. As she turned; I smiled at her and said, "Peace." She just looked at me, in not a very friendly manner, turned away and said something to her friend in a different language. I tapped her on the shoulder for the second time, gave her a big smile and said again, "Peace." All of a sudden her attitude changed. She smiled back and shook her head in agreement. How wonderful is God's grace that helps us to come to peace within ourselves and to reach out to others!

The time dragged on as we waited and I continued to grow more and more tired and fatigued. My legs were starting to feel quite heavy. I tried sitting on the floor of the church but that didn't work either. I got up and decided to offer my suffering in union with Our Lord's suffering during his Passion for the salvation of souls.

Finally, the Pope arrived and proceeded down the aisle to offer Mass on this special day, commemorating the day Our Lord Jesus instituted the Holy Eucharist at the Last Supper, the night before He died. How wonderful it was to be present at the Mass offered by Pope John Paul II on Holy Thursday.

When the time came for Holy Communion and I received Our Lord, I heard within myself, "If you knew what you gained you would jump for joy!" I knew Jesus spoke to me, there was no doubt about it, and I was so filled with joy at that moment that I didn't even care about being tired. In fact, all the tiredness left me! Praise God in the Most Blessed Sacrament!

After Mass we went back to the hotel, and

I was filled with such great gratitude! How generous Our Lord is when we offer our sufferings, no matter how small, in union with His. I am reminded of what Saint Mother Teresa once said, "So much suffering is wasted."

~~~~~~~~~

Several weeks before this pilgrimage began, I received a call from an acquaintance who said she heard we were going over to Italy to see the Shroud of Turin. She said she knew a man who worked for one of the major television stations who wanted to interview someone who was going there. She asked me if I would be willing to have him call me to see if he could set up an interview. Even though the thought of it made me a little nervous, I had to say yes to her because I felt it was an opportunity to witness for Our Lord.

Well, I did get the phone call and an appointment was set up. When a white van pulled up on the scheduled day and time, I couldn't believe what was happening, *me* being interviewed for a television show?! The fellow was very gracious, set up his equipment in my living room, and proceeded to ask me why I wanted to go overseas to view the Shroud, etc. When the interview was over he said, "You'll be hearing from me in a week or so." Within the next couple of weeks he called to say that the TV station had decided not to go ahead with their plans for a segment on the Shroud. I can't say that I was terribly disappointed. I just wanted to do whatever the good Lord wanted me to do.

The second day the Shroud was being shown to the public; our tour bus took us to the place of exposition. As we walked inside the large, dimly lit room, we could see there were wide roped-off aisles where the people were brought to stand as they looked up to view the Holy Cloth. Our group was very fortunate because we had tickets for the second row. As we gazed up at the burial cloth of Jesus, so meticulously spread out on two wide polished wood boards, one holding the cloth that had covered the front of His Divine Body and the other that had covered His back, we were astonished and greatly saddened to see the number of wound marks and blood stains that were imprinted on the cloth. Our Lord Jesus was completely covered with wounds. How many lashes did He have to endure during the scourging to cause all this? How many spikes were on the leather straps that were used by the Roman soldiers? It was heart-wrenching!

Soon we were asked to move on so that the next group of people could take our place. How somber we all were as we left! The Shroud had moved us deeply, to the very core of our being.

As we were leaving the church, there was a television crew interviewing the people on their reaction to what they had just seen. There was a woman in front of me to whom they advanced with a microphone. After saying a few words the interviewer asked if there was anyone else who would like to say something. I just *had* to step forward and share, sadly, how, "Seeing the Shroud made me realize more fully how much Our Lord suffered for us."

Evidently this was the interview Our Lord desired of me, not the one before I had actually seen the burial cloth. He willingly took upon himself the punishment due for our sins, so that we, the guilty ones, could be saved.

There is a very special chapel devoted to the Shroud, with a replica of the burial cloth of Jesus, in the Church of Corpus Christi, in Port Chester, New York. My husband and I have visited there a number of times, and have brought members of our family and friends who were also very much moved by what they saw. Included in the chapel are relics of the Passion of Our Lord that were donated by Pope Pius XII. There is also, in the back of the Church, a large crucifix made according to the wounds found on the Body of Jesus which are represented on the Shroud. My husband Ed feels so moved when looking at this crucifix and praying before it that he says, "It's like going on retreat."

In December of 2011, it was reported from Rome, Italy that a new study on the Shroud of Turin had concluded, after five years of experiments using different methods of coloring linen, that there is no scientific explanation for the image that appears on the cloth (of the Shroud). Italy's National Agency for New Technologies, Energy and Sustainable Economic Development said that the image is not the result of any process known to the modern world. The study indicated that the image may have been created by an intense source of light, but no man-made light would produce the required strength.

~~~~~~~~~

When we visited La Salette, we learned about our Blessed Mother's apparition in 1846 to two young shepherds, Maximin and Melanie. Our Lady told them of the need for holiness of life, especially through daily prayer and respect for the Sabbath (our Sunday obligation). When the children first saw Our Lady she shed tears because of all the work being done in the fields on Sunday, the great neglect on the part of the people to attend Mass except for a few old women, the blasphemy, and the habitual use of Our Lord's name being used irreverently. She told them of chastisements that were coming if people did not come back to God.

My husband and I have been privileged to visit the following Eucharistic miracle sites, and there are a number of others, that Our Lord Jesus has given us to increase our faith in his Divine Presence in the bread and wine that has been consecrated and changed into His Body and Blood by the priest, through the action of the Holy Spirit, during the Holy Sacrifice of the Mass.

Arrangements were made for our group to go to Lanciano, while we were in Italy. Around the year 700 A.D., a Basilian monk was having doubts about the Real Presence of Jesus in the Eucharist. He continued to say Mass begging God to take away his doubt. One day, during Holy Mass, after he said the words of the consecration, "This is My Body"....... "This is My Blood.......," the Host changed into Flesh and the wine changed into real Blood to his great astonishment! Extremely shaken by what God caused to happen before his eyes, he then invited the people that were present to come up to the altar to see what had taken place. The changed substances were not consumed. They were reverently placed in a special container. In 1793, still intact, and as fresh as the day of the transformation, the precious substances were placed in a silver monstrance in which they still can be venerated at the Church of St. Francis in Lanciano.

In 1970, medical experts were requested to decide on the validity of the above acclaimed miracle. After carefully testing the substances they found that the Flesh is real flesh and the Blood, real blood of a human Person. The Flesh is of a heart and the Blood type is AB. They found no preservative, nor has there been one added.

In 1974, the Cardinal of Krakow in Poland, the future Pope John Paul II, visited Lanciano and venerated the Holy Relics. He wrote in the shrine guest register, "Make us always to believe more in You, to have hope in You, and to love You" (Eucharistic Hymn of St. Thomas). Taken from the leaflet BR-28, Association of Marian Helpers, Stockbridge, MA 01263.

Our pilgrimage to Fatima, Portugal, included a visit to the Church of the Holy Miracle in Santarem, not far from Fatima. In that church there is reserved for all to see, (and there are thousands of pilgrims who go there every year), the Eucharistic Miracle which took place in the early 13th century. During that time, a woman was very distraught because her husband was being unfaithful to her. Unfortunately, she visited a sorceress who told her that if she would bring her a Eucharistic Host that was consecrated at the Mass her husband would then become faithful. The woman, though very much afraid, did as the sorceress requested. She went to Mass and received Holy Communion without swallowing the Host. When she got back to her pew she removed the Host from her mouth and placed it in her handkerchief. As she was leaving the church the Host started to bleed. Some of the parishioners noticed, thought she had cut her hand, and tried to help her. The woman hurriedly ran home, and placed the Host in a trunk in her bedroom. Her husband came home late that evening.

During the night a radiant light issuing through the trunk woke them up. Her husband, very startled, asked his wife what could be happening. She confessed to him what she had done and they both knelt down in repentance before the Miracle. In the morning they told their priest what had happened. The priest placed the miraculous Host in a wax container and returned it to the Church of St. Stephen from which it had been taken. Word spread about quickly and many people came to see the miraculous Host. The priest was extremely surprised when he opened the tabernacle where he had placed the encased Host, to see that the wax container was broken and the Host was now in a crystal pyx. It was then placed in a monstrance above the tabernacle, where it can still be seen today. After investigation the Church approved of the miracle and its veneration.

It has also been our privilege to venerate in the Basilica of St. Francis in Siena, Italy another marvelous miracle of the Eucharist. On August 14, 1730 thieves broke into the tabernacle of the Church and stole the ciborium that contained consecrated Hosts. The theft was not discovered until the next morning during the Holy Sacrifice of the Mass when the priest opened the tabernacle door to distribute Holy Communion to the people. Public prayers of reparation were ordered by the Archbishop. Two days later a priest noticed something white at the opening of the poor box at the church of St. Mary of Provenzano. When the box was opened it was found to contain the Hosts that were missing from the Church of St. Francis. Since the Hosts became covered with dust and cobwebs that were in the receptacle for alms, they were not consumed. They were cleaned off and were expected to deteriorate over a period of time. At that stage Christ would no longer be present. Instead the Hosts have remained fresh, with a pleasing scent of unleavened bread, for over 250 years. And on May 29, 1954, while he was still the Patriarch of Venice, the future Pope John XXIII signed the book of visitors and venerated the miraculous Hosts.

The Hosts have been examined and tested and it has been determined that their preservation is extraordinary. In order that the faithful may venerate the miraculous Hosts, they are enclosed in glass surrounded by an ornate container. I still remember, when kneeling before this wonderful miracle, how very white and perfect the Hosts were, even though more than 250 years have passed since they were consecrated.

What a wonderful awe inspiring pilgrimage it turned out to be!

SAINT PIO OF PIETRELCINA

Saint Pio (Padre Pio) as many still affectionately call him, was born in Pietrelcina, Italy in 1887 and was ordained a priest, a Capuchin Franciscan Friar, in 1910. While praying before the Crucifix after Mass in 1918 the five wounds of Our Lord Jesus Christ, (the stigmata) were visibly seen in his hands, feet and side. For some years before this time he had the pain of the wounds, which were at that time invisible. He bore these wounds of Our Lord Jesus for 50 years. He regularly bled up to a pint of blood from his hands every Friday, and he offered all this pain for the salvation of souls.

The Lord God gave him supernatural gifts: the gift of healing and the gift of reading souls were among them. Having the gift of reading souls enabled Fr. Pio to read into the heart and conscience of people in order to guide them to conversion and to a closer union with God. Many people from all over the world visited San Giovanni Rotondo where he lived at Our Lady of Grace Capuchin Friary, to be present at his daily Mass and to confess their sins to this holy priest from whom they received much spiritual help and guidance.

St. Pio had a great devotion to his guardian angel and encouraged everyone to appreciate the constant help of his or her guardian angel who is always there to guide and protect us.

A number of years ago when Fr. Gérard J. Breault, O.M.V. came to visit Ed and me in Yonkers, we decided to go to the Medjugorje prayer group in New Rochelle that was held in the home of the teaching Brothers across the street from Iona High School. It was arranged ahead of time that Fr. Breault would offer the Holy Sacrifice of the Mass there. The prayer group was held once a month in the evening.

When we arrived the driveway of the Brother's house was already filled with cars, so Ed parked in the parking lot of Iona Prep. Fr. Breault and I walked ahead and my husband followed with Father's suitcase that contained his Mass kit. All of a sudden I heard the piercing sound of car brakes screeching to a halt! I turned around to see my Ed on the pavement, beginning to get up. I ran over to him. "I'm all right, I'm all right," he kept saying as he picked up Father's case and continued to cross the street to the meeting. I said, "Wait a minute, we need to get the license, etc. of the person that hit you. Ed would hear none of it as he continued on. In the meantime I turned to the driver of the car that hit Ed.

He was an elderly man who was driving home with his wife. The poor man was shaking all over. He kept saying, "I thought I killed him, I thought I killed him." I couldn't help but try to console the distraught man and his wife. I put my arms around him, patted him on the back and kept telling him that my husband says he's all right. I was afraid he was going to have a heart attack, he was so upset! So there I was, comforting the man who hit my husband while Ed was on his way to join the prayer group! It sure did make for a good story later whenever we talked about what happened!

Finally the driver and I decided to exchange phone numbers so that we could call each other to confirm how Ed was feeling. All Ed suffered was a scratch on his cheek which I washed with soap. Ed said the washing with soap hurt him more than being hit by the car!! And so, we then celebrated a beautiful Mass followed by the prayers and sharing of the prayer group.

Later Ed told us when he was hit by the car he felt no pain! He had this feeling of floating in the air going up and then a feeling of floating as he came down!! He has often said he keeps his guardian angel working overtime! He is sure it was his angel who kept him from getting hurt.

Praise God for his gift to us of, "an angelic spirit who never leaves us for an instant from the cradle to the grave, who guides and protects us like a friend or a brother…" (Padre Pio in a letter to Raffaelina Cerase, April 20, 1915.)*

Prayer to our Guardian Angel

Angel of God, my guardian dear, to whom God's love commits me here. Ever this day be at my side, to light and guard, to rule and guide. Amen.

*From Quiet Moments with Padre Pio, 120 Daily Readings, compiled by Patricia Treece. Servants, an Imprint of Franciscan Media. Used with permission.

~~~~~~~~~~

When we invited the prayer group we were part of when we lived in Yonkers for a cookout at our home in Connecticut, we sat around the table in our dining area after dinner and shared some stories. Here is one of them.

A few years ago, shortly after retiring, one of our friends, Dolores, suffered a severe attack of sciatica. After undergoing months of physical therapy, cortisone treatments and trying multiple pain killers, she still had excruciating pain. As a last resort she decided to have surgery.

The operation was successful, but required months of recuperation. She was unable to drive and sorely missed attending daily Mass. On Sundays she and her husband went to church together, so she was able to go to Mass with him because he was the driver.

One day a friend gave Dolores a St. Pio Mass card for healing. She decided to include in her prayers the novena to the Sacred Heart of Jesus that was on the card. Padre Pio prayed this novena every day for those who asked for his prayers. For about two months she prayed this special prayer. Upon arising one morning she said to herself, "I'm tired of this. I'm going to drive myself to the nine o'clock Mass."

Although she was nervous about it, she decided to take the chance and drive to the church which was close by. When she arrived at Mass, she opened the Missal provided at church to the Mass for that day. She was astonished to see it was the feast day of St. Pio, (September 23)! It was then that she realized St. Pio had also prayed to the Sacred Heart for her and she's been driving ever since!

This is the novena prayer to the Sacred Heart of Jesus recited every day by Padre Pio for all those who asked for his prayers.

I. O my Jesus, You have said: "Truly I say to you, ask and it will be given you, seek and you will find, knock and it will be opened to you." Behold, I knock, I seek, and I ask for the grace of...
Our Father..., Hail Mary..., Glory be to the Father...
Sacred Heart of Jesus, I place all my trust in You.

II. O my Jesus, You have said: "Truly I say to you, if you ask anything of the Father in My Name, He will give it to you." Behold, in Your name, I ask the Father for the grace of...

Our Father..., Hail Mary..., Glory be to the Father...
Sacred Heart of Jesus, I place all my trust in You.

III. O my Jesus, You have said: "Truly I say to you, heaven and earth will pass away, but My words will not pass away." Encouraged by Your infallible words I now ask for the grace of...
Our Father..., Hail Mary..., Glory be to the Father...
Sacred Heart of Jesus, I place all my trust in You.

O Sacred Heart of Jesus, for whom it is impossible not to have compassion on the afflicted, have mercy on us sinners, and grant us the grace which we ask of You, through the Sorrowful and Immaculate Heart of Mary, Your tender mother and ours.

Say the Hail, Holy Queen prayer...

Conclude with: St. Joseph, foster father of Jesus, pray for us.

(Novena taken from the leaflet printed by the Capuchin Franciscan Friars, P.O. Box 839, Union City, N.J. 07087 Phone 201-863-4036).

For those who wish to contact the Friary where St. Pio lived for over fifty years:

Our Lady of Grace Capuchin Friary 71013, San Giovanni Rotondo, FG, Italy

From Padre Pio: "But remember, I can do much more for you from Heaven than I can do for you on earth." "Pray, hope and don't worry." "Anxiety doesn't help at all. Our merciful Lord will listen to your prayer." "Abandon yourself to the Sacred Heart of Jesus and let Him take care of everything."

Padre Pio died on September 23, 1968 and was canonized a saint by Pope John Paul II on June 16, 2002. He and St. Teresa of Calcutta were great promoters of the Miraculous Medal. They gave blessed medals to many and when St. Pio passed away the friars found some medals still in his pocket.

SAINT ANTHONY OF PADUA

A couple of years ago our son-in-law Bill telephoned me to share his story about St. Anthony. He told me his wife Elizabeth, who is our daughter, always prayed to St. Anthony whenever she couldn't find something. He said she had great faith in his ability to answer her prayers. Bill, not being Catholic, was not drawn in any way to pray to St. Anthony to help him find something that was lost, (although a number of Christians of other faiths have found that St. Anthony's prayers are very efficacious for finding a lost article).

Well, one day Bill, no matter how hard he looked, could not find his cell phone charger. He decided to give St. Anthony a try and prayed that he would help him find it. As he went around the house opening drawers, etc., he became more and more surprised as he began finding one thing after another; items that had been lost for quite some time, in places where he had already looked even that very morning! Although he still hadn't found his cell phone charger, he began laughing with joy at the message he felt he was receiving and was grateful for finding all the other items. As he started to leave the house he felt that St. Anthony was probably making a point with him to see how easy this sort of thing is when one knows that Our Lord, the angels and the saints are there to help. Bill experienced a great relief and joy at that message.

Immediately upon having that thought, he was then inspired to check another place and found his cell phone charger! He was so excited he had to call me up and tell me all about it. We both rejoiced in the power of prayers to St. Anthony. No wonder he is often called the patron saint of lost articles.

~~~~~~~~~~

One of our friends, Debra, shared the following story.

As a realtor I spend a good part of my day moving from location to location. I started out on a normal day driving to my first project, an open house. After driving a half-hour I stopped to purchase coffee and doughnuts to offer hospitality to those who would arrive. Then I stopped at several intersections to place my open house signs that are used for directions and advertisement. Since it had snowed it was a little more difficult than usual. When I returned to my car after placing the signs, I noticed the diamond was missing from my wedding ring!

This year was especially important to me since it was our 40th wedding anniversary. The diamond was given to me by my husband as a gift that he purchased while in South Africa, thirty years ago, and I have a lot of memories surrounding his thoughtful, unexpected present. And of course, it was a monetary loss as well. I became extremely upset, and I couldn't get the loss out of my mind and my day was only beginning!

When I arrived at my open house the home owners noticed how upset I was and asked me what was wrong. After telling my story they immediately started praying to Saint Anthony and advised me to do the same.

After a full day's work which included driving to my appointments and putting about 100 miles on the road, I was on my way home. Now, with nothing else on my mind, I began to recap the start of my day. Where could I possibly have lost my diamond!? Was it still somewhere at home? Did I lose it getting in and out of the car when I put out the signs? I just had no idea!

For some reason I went back to the doughnut store to look. It was a 20-mile trip out of my way but something made me go there without giving it much thought. The moment I walked in my eyes looked down at the carpet. It was covered with sand and rock salt that could also have the appearance of a diamond. But there it was, sparkling and shining up at me like it was the only thing on the floor! I was in awe and speechless as I picked it up and walked out. *Thank you Saint Anthony.*

When I arrived home I told my husband that the diamond found its way back to me, and it was all because of my customers' prayers to Saint Anthony. I was thankful for their suggestion that I pray to him also. Then my husband told me of his day of searching our home for the diamond which also included taking the sink drains apart. He said that when I called to tell him of my misfortune, he was just leaving our parish church. Without giving it any thought he turned around, went back to light a candle and prayed to Saint Anthony.

Our hearts were filled with gratitude and praise, to Our Lord and Saint Anthony.

~~~~~~~~

Saint Anthony was born in Lisbon in

1195. At a young age he joined the Augustinians, although the date of his ordination to the priesthood is not known. In the year 1220 he was present when the remains of the first Franciscan martyrs who were put to death in Morroco, were returned to Coimbre. He was then inflamed with a desire for martyrdom in the service of Our Lord Jesus and decided to enter the Order of Friars Minor (the Franciscans), and it was there that he acquired the name of Anthony. His desire to live and preach in Morroco was not able to be fulfilled since he became severely ill soon after he arrived there and he was eventually shipped back home. Because of a violent storm at sea the ship landed on the coast of Sicily. After some time he regained his health there.

On the ordination day of a number of Dominicans and Franciscans, it was discovered that no one was appointed to give the sermon. And no one wanted to take on that responsibility unprepared. Anthony was chosen and hesitantly accepted. No one present expected to hear the depth and powerful insight of the sermon that Anthony delivered with the help of the Holy Spirit!

St. Francis, having heard of him as a great

man of prayer and a great Scripture and theology scholar, asked him in a letter to teach theology to the friars, "…provided, however, that as the Rule prescribes, the spirit of prayer and devotion may not be extinguished." Eventually he was called to preach in Italy and France where he brought about numerous conversions to the faith.

Many miracles occurred because of the prayers of this holy friar. One day he was served poisoned food by some heretics, which he rendered harmless by the sign of the cross. On another occasion he preached at the river's edge and the fish jumped out of the water to hear him! (It has been said that this is what Anthony did on a day when the people wouldn't listen to him, because they were afraid of being converted, his speeches were so convincing, and they didn't want to be converted…and so, the fish eagerly listened to him!) There were thousands of others however who came to hear him. The crowds were so great that the churches could not hold them, so he went to the piazzas or to the open fields. After his talks he and the friars would hear the confessions of the people.

Friar Anthony died on June 13, 1231 at the age of thirty-six. Pope Gregory IX declared him a saint within a year after his death, being convinced of his sanctity and persuaded by the many miracles that had occurred through his intercession. He was declared a Doctor of the Church by Pope Pius XII in 1946.

Prayer to St. Anthony

O holy St. Anthony, gentlest of saints, your love for God and charity for His creatures, made you worthy to possess miraculous powers. Miracles waited on your word, which you are ever ready to speak for those in trouble or anxiety. Encouraged by this thought, I implore you to obtain for me (make your request). The answer to my prayer may require a miracle; even so you are the saint of miracles. O gentle and loving St. Anthony, whose heart was ever full of human sympathy, whisper my petition into the ears of the sweet Infant Jesus, who loved to be held in your arms; and the gratitude of my heart will ever be yours. Amen. Our Father, Hail Mary and Glory be.

Note: Story of the life of St. Anthony of Padua was obtained from a variety of sources.

THE HOLY LAND

What a gift it was to go to the Holy Land to visit the grace-filled places where Jesus Our Lord was born, raised and walked on the face of this earth. Our friends and former neighbors, Jane and Jack Devaney had moved to Florida, and during a telephone conversation Jane told me she and Jack were going on a pilgrimage to the Holy Land. Their plane was leaving from Fort Myers, then up to JFK International Airport in New York to transfer to the plane that would take them overseas. I decided to ask Ed if he thought we could join the pilgrimage when they arrived at JFK, if it was all right with Jane and Jack and the sponsors of the trip. Ed agreed and so did our friends and those involved with the arrangements. How happy I was!

In the morning we began our pilgrimage. A Franciscan priest met our group to be our guide and offer Mass for us at all the holy sites. The Order of Friars Minor (the Franciscans) have been present in the Holy Land since the 13th century, "to look after, restore and protect the Holy Places of Christianity." (Paul VI-Nobis in animo, 1974) They followed the visit of St. Francis who went to the Holy Land in 1217.

How special it was to visit the Basilica of the Annunciation in Nazareth. Inside the church is the place where the Angel Gabriel having been sent by God, announced to the Virgin Mary that she was to become the Mother of Jesus, through the power of the Holy Spirit. In the lower church there is a grotto where, upon the wall an inscription in Greek proclaims, "This is the Holy Place of Mary." How moving it was to be and pray at this holy site where the Son of God came down from heaven and was made flesh in the womb of the most Blessed Virgin Mary.

Upon hearing from the angel that her elderly cousin Elizabeth was also expecting a child, *"...for nothing will be impossible for God"* (Luke 1:37), Mary visited Elizabeth and stayed with her for about three months. We were brought to the Church of the Visitation where the home of Elizabeth and Zachariah was blessed by the visit of the Virgin Mary and the Infant Jesus present in her womb.

We were taken for a boat ride on the Sea of Galilee, saw the remains of a temple which had been built over the site of the temple where Jesus preached in Capernaum, but nothing was as special to us as visiting the place of Jesus' birth in Bethlehem and the site of the Crucifixion of Our Lord on Calvary.

When our group arrived at the Church of the Nativity in Bethlehem, we were taken to the entrance, which is a low opening in the wall of the Church where we had to bend down in order to enter. Centuries ago the church was built this way in order to prevent those who wanted to destroy it from entering into it on their horses. We had to descend a number of steps to the spot where Jesus was born. Greek Orthodox priests were there praying when we arrived at this special site. How thankful and blessed we were to be here to offer our love and prayers to Our Lord Jesus. On the opposite wall behind glass there was a beautiful statue of the Infant Jesus. As I was looking at it, I thought of how His little hands, feet, and heart would eventually be pierced in atonement for our sins. After a time spent in prayer we proceeded up the stairs to the main church for Mass.

On one of our trips to the Holy Land we stayed overnight at a hotel in Tiberias. The hotel was built very close to and overlooked the Sea of Galilee. What a beautiful view to behold the Sea of Galilee, the same sea as it was when Jesus sailed on it with His disciples over 2,000 years ago! The same sea Jesus walked on to meet His disciples after He had stayed behind to pray alone in the hills, while they had gone on ahead in the boat. It meant a lot to Ed.

During the night a great storm blew up on the lake. (The Sea of Galilee is also called Lake Gennesaret). I was awakened from my sleep as I heard windows in the room rattling vehemently. I was startled as I imagined that the water just *had* to be very close and maybe would enter the room! I got up and looked out the window. The wind and waves were very strong but thank goodness the water was still far from us.

In the morning at breakfast everyone was talking about the tremendous storm and we recalled the scripture reading when Jesus was asleep in a boat with some of His disciples on the Sea of Galilee.

"A violent squall came up and waves were breaking over the boat, so that it was already filling up. Jesus was in the stern, asleep on a cushion. They woke him and said to him, 'Teacher, do you not care that we are perishing?' He woke up, rebuked the wind, and said to the sea, 'Quiet! Be still!' The wind ceased and there was great calm. Then he asked them, 'Why are you terrified? Do you not

yet have faith?' They were filled with great awe and said to one another, 'Who then is this whom even wind and sea obey?'" (Mark 4:37-41)

We had first-hand experience the night before of just how fearful Jesus' disciples must have been while in a boat in such a violent windstorm.

A memorable sight for us was the Wailing Wall, or Western Wall as the Jewish people call it, one of the retaining walls of the Temple Mount, where they weep and pray over the loss of their temple which was destroyed by the Romans in 70 A.D.

Men and women are separated to pray at different areas of the wall. Men, who are required to wear yarmulkes or some other head covering, which was provided if they had no hat, prayed at the left side of the wall and the women at the right. There were openings in between many of the blocks of the wall where pilgrims would put their intentions which were written on paper and placed in the openings. It was something to see the many openings that were filled with papers protruding out from the wall.

I prayed the Rosary with my forehead

touching the wall, and just as I finished our group was called to the bus. I remember how Jesus was brought to the temple by Mary and Joseph to be presented to God the Father, so praying at this wall was very meaningful for me. So often while I'm praying the Joyful Mysteries of the Rosary and come to the fourth decade, the Presentation of the child Jesus in the Temple, I remember being at the Wailing Wall and offer once again the intentions that I placed there, and all the intentions that have ever been offered at that holy site. How happy we were to see, on television, Pope John Paul II visiting, praying, and placing his intentions in the same wall when he visited the Holy Land. Later Pope Benedict XVI and then Pope Francis did the same.

At Cana in Galilee, the priest led those of us who were married in the renewal of our wedding vows. This was where Our Lord performed His first public miracle of changing water into wine after His mother said to Him, "They have no wine."

"... [There] was a wedding in Cana in Galilee, and the mother of Jesus was there. Jesus and his disciples were also invited to the wedding. When the wine ran short, the mother

*of Jesus said to him, 'They have no wine.'
[And] Jesus said to her, 'Woman, how does
your concern affect me? My hour has not yet
come.' His mother said to the servers, 'Do
whatever he tells you.' Now there were six stone
water jars there for Jewish ceremonial
washings, each holding twenty to thirty gallons.
Jesus told them, 'Fill the jars with water.' So
they filled them to the brim. Then he told them,
'Draw some out now and take it to the
headwaiter.' So they took it. And when the
headwaiter tasted the water that had become
wine, without knowing where it came from
(although the servers who had drawn the water
knew), the headwaiter called the bridegroom
and said to him, 'Everyone serves good wine
first, and then when people have drunk freely,
an inferior one; but you have kept the good
wine until now.' Jesus did this as the beginning
of his signs in Cana in Galilee and so revealed
his glory, and his disciples began to believe in
him."* (John 2:1-11)

The Pater Noster Church, (Our Father in
Latin), is located on the Mount of Olives,
tradition believing it stands on the site where
Jesus taught his disciples how to pray. I couldn't

help hoping that there would eventually be many more churches named in the world after Our Father, because I don't know of any other than this one in the Holy Land, do you?

We pilgrims walked along the "Via Dolorosa," in Jesus' footsteps on the way to Calvary. "Stations," places of prayer to stop at and pray, are there at intervals on the way. We stopped at each station and prayed as a group with our priest. The Stations of the Cross which are in our Catholic Churches are there as a reminder to us of Our Lord Jesus' suffering and death and to help us to meditate and pray about all He willingly endured for our salvation.

When we arrived at the Church of the Holy Sepulcher, which encompasses the scene of the Crucifixion of Our Lord and also the tomb of His burial and Resurrection, we were so grateful to be and to pray in so holy a place which Our Lord Himself sanctified by the shedding of His blood.

The altar on Calvary is in front of a large Crucifix depicting Our Lord Jesus crucified, with the Blessed Mother on the left and St. John on the right. Further to the right behind a glass encasement, there is a sculpture of Mary, our Blessed Mother with a sword through her

Immaculate Heart as was prophesied by Simeon, at the presentation of Our Lord in the temple when He was an infant. How saddened our hearts were at witnessing this whole scene.

Underneath the altar there is an opening in the marble floor where the pilgrims are allowed to reach down and touch the place where Jesus was crucified. There is a glass window on the floor to the left of the altar where one can see clearly the white rock, "the place of the skull" where the crucifixion took place. On our last visit to the Holy Land, Ed and I knelt down under the altar and touched this holy spot together.

When we arrived at Calvary, the first time we went to the Holy Land, there were a number of pilgrims there and so we only had a short time to pray and meditate before we had to move on. We were very sad we didn't have more time to spend at such a sacred spot.

Our Franciscan priest offered Holy Mass for us pilgrims in the Catholic chapel within the Church of the Holy Sepulcher. How very special it was for us to be there; for the Church teaches that the Mass is the same sacrifice as the sacrifice of Jesus on the Cross. He intercedes for us, as He offers Himself in an unbloody manner, under the appearances of bread and wine, to God the

Father in reparation for our sins. At every Mass we attend we are present at Calvary. "The Eucharist is thus a sacrifice because it *re-presents* (makes present) the sacrifice of the cross, because it is its *memorial* and because it *applies* its fruit:..." (Catechism of the Catholic Church # 1366)

The Last Supper.

"When the hour came, he took his place at table with the apostles. He said to them, "I have eagerly desired to eat this Passover with you before I suffer, for, I tell you, I shall not eat it [again] until there is fulfillment in the kingdom of God." Then he took a cup, gave thanks, and said, "Take this and share it among yourselves; for I tell you [that] from this time on I shall not drink of the fruit of the vine until the kingdom of God comes." Then he took the bread, said the blessing, broke it, and gave it to them, saying, "This is my body, which will be given for you; do this in memory of me." And likewise the cup after they had eaten, saying, "This cup is the new covenant in my blood, which will be shed for you." (Luke 22:14-20)

"That in this sacrament are the true Body of Christ and His true Blood is something that 'cannot be apprehended by the senses', says St. Thomas, 'but *only by faith*, which relies on divine authority.' For this reason, in a commentary on *Luke* 22:19 ('This is my body which is given for you.'), St. Cyril says: 'Do not doubt whether this is true, but rather receive the words of the Savior in faith, for since he is the truth, he cannot lie.'" (Catechism #1381)[1]

In this chapel, at a side altar, there is a large piece of the pillar at which Jesus was scourged. One could sense the great suffering He endured there for us.

"But he was pierced for our offences, crushed for our sins. Upon Him was the chastisement that makes us whole, by his stripes we were healed." (Isaiah 53:5)

Only a few of us at a time entered the tomb of the burial and Resurrection of Jesus as the tomb was quite small. There was a priest present inside to assist the people and to remind

---

[1] St. Thomas Aquinas, *STh* III, 75,1; cf. Paul VI, *MF 18;* St. Cyril of Alexandria, *In Luc.* 22, 19: PG 72, 912; cf. Paul VI, *MF* 18.

them when it was time to leave to make room for other pilgrims. Candles were provided for those who wished to light one at Calvary or at the tomb. Before we left home, one of our friends had asked us to purchase a candle to be placed on Calvary for her intentions, which we did. We also had one lit there and outside the tomb as well for all our intentions.

Our hotel was located outside the city wall but very close to the gate that led to the Via Dolorosa and Calvary. Ed and I decided that the next day, which was a free day for us we would go back again to visit and pray at Calvary. The following day, as we walked out of the elevator on the main floor, a maid was passing by pushing a cart with a number of roses, each in its own vase, on top of the cart. I remarked how beautiful the roses were and was surprised when she asked me if I would like one. How happy I was to say, "Yes," because then I could bring our rose to Calvary.

When we entered the Church of the Holy Sepulcher and climbed the stairs to the Crucifixion scene, there was no one there except a religious Sister who was taking care of the chapel. I gave her our rose and she put it with the other flowers along the wall to the left of the altar.

Ed motioned to me to come back a little further where he was kneeling and praying. He had found a spot on the marble floor which was smoothly indented, where many thousands of pilgrims must have previously knelt there praying. Together we softly prayed the Sorrowful Mysteries of the Rosary.

More pilgrims soon arrived but we were able to continue to stay where we were because we were in no one's way. How blessed we felt to have that additional time on Calvary.

Site of the Annunciation of the Angel Gabriel to Mary that she was to become the Mother of Jesus, the Son of God

Site of the Nativity of the Infant Jesus in Bethlehem

*At the Site of the Crucifixion of Jesus in the Church
of the Holy Sepulchre*

Sculpture of the Immaculate Heart of Mary pierced with a sword

Pilgrims praying at the Wailing Wall

The Sea of Galilee at sunset

Some years later our parish priest, Fr. Patrick Walsh, S.M.A. planned a pilgrimage to the Holy Land, Egypt and a two night stay in Athens, Greece that would give us an opportunity to see the Acropolis which dates back to the 5th century B.C. We decided to go and we were not disappointed. It was wonderful to be back in the Holy Land! We stayed a couple of nights in a hotel on a mountain across from the one Jerusalem was built on. And so, when we were in the dining room which had large glass windows, we could look across and see the Church of the Holy Sepulchre, the Dome of the Rock, and so much of Jerusalem. It was breathtaking!

It is 264 miles from Jerusalem to Cairo, Egypt. It was quite a long but worthwhile ride by bus. Only then did we appreciate the sufferings that Mary, Joseph and the child Jesus endured during their flight into Egypt to save Jesus from King Herod's order to massacre all Hebrew infants two years of age and under so that Jesus would be slain.

The road we traveled was very narrow and sand was everywhere. Depending on the wind, the sand was flying all around us. We had to stop at a small station in the middle of the desert to await a different bus to take us further into Egypt. There was an overhead fan but it was still very hot and we had a long wait as there was trouble in the area at that time.

We were given the opportunity to ride on a boat through the Suez Canal and visit the Pyramids which we had read about so many years ago in grammar school. We also saw the church that is considered the oldest church in Egypt, St. Sergius, which dates back to the 4th century. According to tradition the church was built on the spot where the Holy Family, Mary, Joseph and the child Jesus rested on their journey and may have lived for some time during their stay in Egypt.

The third and last time we visited the Holy Land was in November, 2008. We had received in the mail a flyer about a twelve-day pilgrimage sponsored by Our Sorrowful Mother's Ministry with Father Mark Baron, M.I.C. (Marians of the Immaculate Conception) as chaplain. Ed and I have a special love in our hearts for the Marians and their wonderful National Shrine of the Divine Mercy in Stockbridge, Massachusetts. It is from there that they spread the message of Divine Mercy and also devotion to our Blessed Mother Mary. Therefore we decided to sign up for the trip.

One of our friends, Wilma DiFiore, from our former Marriage Encounter group, happened to call me around this time, and as we were talking I mentioned that Ed and I were going to the Holy Land. She said, *"You're going to the Holy Land?"* Yes," I replied. "Do you want to come?" "Yes," she answered. Even though they had been there six times before, she was very excited about joining us. And so, she and her husband, Deacon Augustine DiFiore also signed up for the pilgrimage. How good it was to have them with us! It was amazing that she called us at that particular time, because we hadn't been in touch with each other for quite a while.

Then, guess what? Ed started having heart trouble and needed to have two stents inserted to rectify his problem. And this was only one month before the scheduled trip! We asked the cardiologist if he thought Ed would be able to leave a month later with the pilgrimage. He said we'd have to see how he was doing.

I made a phone call to Debbie Pryor of Our Sorrowful Mother's Ministry and asked her to pray with me for Ed's healing, which she did. She also put Ed's name on the prayer list. About a week before the pilgrimage the doctor gave his okay and off we went. Ed did beautifully, thank God! We were both surprised that he was doing better than some of the other men as we walked up hill to visit one of the churches.

On this pilgrimage Fr. Baron arranged to have a Holy Hour in Adoration of the Blessed Sacrament every day when possible. We also had prayers for healing for those who wished to be prayed over. Our hotel in Tiberias was situated on the Sea of Galilee. Father arranged to have a table set up covered with a white cloth and candles, very close to and overlooking the water that first night we were there for Mass. How magnificent it was to have Mass at night, with candles glowing, followed by a Holy Hour and prayers for healing before the Blessed Sacrament, overlooking the Sea of Galilee!

How happy I was when we were brought by bus to King David's tomb, who of course, wrote the Psalms. After we prayed and left the site, an Israeli soldier, who was very friendly to us, consented to having his picture taken with us and the DiFiores.

Many years ago my Aunt Alma shared with me how much she loved reading the Psalms. Because of her sharing I began to open to the Psalms every morning and would read one or two of them and was very much encouraged by them. Later, I also added turning to the New Testament for a "word for the day," after a prayer to be guided by the Holy Spirit, which I also did before I opened to a Psalm. How often I was most grateful to where I was led because of the encouragement I received.

One day, after noticing for quite some time a stack of "Shorter Christian Prayer" books in one of our local churches that were obviously there for those who participated in these prayers in common before Mass, I decided to purchase one of these books and began to pray "Morning Prayer" which eventually led to including "Evening Prayer" also. These prayers are part of the Liturgy of the Hours, which is the prayer of the Catholic Church recited by priests, deacons, religious and a number of lay people throughout the world. The Psalms are also included in these prayers.

According to a Catholic News Service article published in July 2011, Pope Benedict XVI was reported as saying that the Book of Psalms from the Old Testament is a timeless and powerful "prayer book" that teaches Christians how to communicate with God. The 150 "inspired songs" were originally gathered by the Jewish people, but were prophetic of the coming of Jesus Christ, the pope said on June 21, 2011 at the weekly general audience in St. Peter's Square. He said the prayers from the Book of Psalms were used by Jesus himself, "thus revealing their full and profound meaning."

Everyone can relate to the complex and often contradictory expressions of the human condition found in the Psalms, the pope said, citing "joy and suffering, desire for God and feelings of unworthiness, happiness and sense of abandonment, faith in God and painful solitude, fullness of life and fear of death." The pope said that the prayers in the book of Psalms showed the inseparable intertwining of supplication, laments and praise. Believers pray to God lamenting a condition but asking for intercession, knowing they will be heard by a good and merciful God, the pope said. Prayers of praise are offered when supplications have been answered or confessions received with forgiveness, he said. How happy I was to read in the Florida Catholic newspaper some of the thoughts of Pope Benedict XVI on the Psalms.

On this particular trip our group was given a large cross to be carried along with us as we walked and prayed along the Via Dolorosa. Arrangements were made for Fr. Baron to offer Mass on Calvary one morning, at the altar just to the right of the Crucifixion scene. Behind the altar there is a painting of Jesus stretched out on the cross before the cross was raised up. Our Mass was scheduled for five o'clock in the morning, but we didn't mind rising early when we were given such a privilege to attend Mass so close to the place of the Crucifixion of Our Lord. It was very special.

The Holy Land is truly a holy land! How thankful we are to God for all the blessings we received and for giving us the opportunity to go. Visiting there will be etched in our minds and hearts forever.

"Great is the LORD and wholly to be praised /
in the city of our God. / His holy mountain, /
fairest of heights, / is the joy of all the earth..."
Psalm 48:2-3

"For from Zion shall go forth instruction, /
and the word of the LORD from Jerusalem"
(Isaiah 2:3)

EPILOGUE

Dear Reader,

I hope these stories have lifted your spirits and encouraged you to believe in the merciful love of Our Lord Jesus Christ and His Blessed Mother Mary who care for and love each one of us. Jesus is there, waiting at the door of our hearts for our permission to enter, to help us and to give us His peace.

Bishop Fulton J. Sheen once said that Dismas, the "good thief" crucified next to Jesus, "...was a thief to the end! He stole Heaven!!" But why wait until our last breath when we can walk with Jesus now and receive graces, mercy, blessings and salvation for ourselves and others?

At the Holy Sacrifice of the Mass Jesus prays to God our Father for all of us. May the Holy Spirit guide each one of us to everlasting life.

Jacqueline E. Goin

"Show me the way in which I should walk, for to you I lift up my soul. Rescue me from my enemies, O Lord, for in you I hope."

(Psalm 143:8,9)

"O Lord, you mete out peace to us, for it is you who have accomplished all we have done."

(Isaiah 26:12)

"Give thanks to the Lord, acclaim his name; among the nations make known his deeds...."

(Isaiah 12:4)

Made in the USA
Middletown, DE
11 September 2020

18304725R00195